Quality of Service in Modern Packet Networks

First Edition

Gary Hallberg

First Printing, 2019

ISBN-9781690728115

Acknowledgement

I'd like to thank my wife Sarah for proofreading this work, particularly as she freely admits she had no prior knowledge of the technicalities and acronyms it contains. Without her help, this book would most likely not be completed.

Table of Contents

Foreword

Integrated digital networks are ubiquitous in all modern telecommunications infrastructure. Driven by the need to reduce costs whilst enhancing customer experience, there is a constant drive within Service Providers to digitize traditional analogue based technologies and transport them over packet-based networks. The desire is for just one packet network to transport all applications. Packet based technologies are not the best for delivering real time applications like voice, or loss-sensitive applications like video. However, only packet-based technologies provide the low cost and scalability needed to meet today's high bandwidth demands.

From the early days of packet networks, their limitations were well understood and this led to many technological developments to address these shortcomings.

In this book I set out to provide the reader with an understanding of the key technologies developed to deliver Quality of Service (QoS) within packet networks. I address the developments in chronological order, and this historical context provides a deeper understanding of the subject. It also helps explain why some technologies have taken hold and why some have waned.

The book starts by explaining the difference between Circuit Switched and Packet Switched technologies. Some applications are best suited to Circuit Switched networks and do not migrate well to Packet Switched networks. The book explains how some Circuit Switched networks have inherent QoS mechanisms built into the technology and explains the limitations of early packet networks.

All the major approaches to applying QoS in Layer 3 packet networks are explained. In addition, we must be aware that Layer 2 networks are being deployed in greater scale, especially with the advent of standardized Carrier Ethernet technologies.

There is currently a step change in the way networks are being deployed. In this new world of network transformation, we are moving toward Software Defined Networks. Traditional network functions, such as switches and routers, are being virtualized in software and the need for traditional edge routers is being challenged. SD-WAN is one such application challenging the status quo and is a technology that is now widely adopted by service providers. SD-WAN brings a whole new approach to QoS and we will cover these too.

Telecommunications Service Providers have specific challenges when delivering QoS over their networks and the book covers traffic engineering in some detail, including the new technology of Segment Routing.

Delivering Quality of Service in packet networks is only part of the problem. Particularly in carrier environments, there will be a need to measure that Quality of Service against a Service Level Agreement. I have devoted a chapter to looking at such technologies.

I have written this book for the reader with no previous experience of how Quality of Service is delivered in modern networks and it provides enough depth of knowledge for both the student and professional alike. However, the book does assume that the reader has a basic understanding of Ethernet and Packet technologies. For those new to computer networking, I have included a chapter at the start of the book that introduces the novice reader to key technologies needed to understand modern networking. Although not comprehensive, this chapter will provide a solid foundation for further study.

I hope you find this book useful and thank you for taking the time to read it.

Gary Hallberg B.Eng. (hons), M.Phil.

Chapter 1: Network Basics for Review

The topic of QoS within Packet Switched networks can be a complex one and so it is assumed that the reader already understands the fundamentals of Packet Switched technologies. This book is written in such a way that this knowledge is assumed. So as not to exclude the reader who lacks the knowledge of data networking fundamentals, this chapter is included to provide a solid understanding of modern network technologies. It can also help reinforce existing skills and provide some context to later chapters. If you feel you have a good understanding of data networking, then skip this chapter.

The Open Standard Interconnection (OSI) Seven Layer model

If you are looking to get a start in data communications and networking, then this is a good place to begin. Arguably, the Open Standard Interconnection (OSI) seven-layer model is the foundation of computer internetworking. The OSI model has been around since the 1970s and it serves us as well today as it did back then. Having said that, the

OSI model is being challenged by some up and coming technologies, such as Software Defined Networking (SDN) and Network Functions Virtualization (NFV).

The purpose of the OSI model is to make the implementation of computer networks much simpler and to promote standardization. It represents the functions that are needed to deliver a computer network from the application layer to the physical transmission medium. The OSI model or OSI stack comprises seven functional layers. An underlying principle is that the interface between the layers is standardized, but a variety of technologies can be used to realize the layer itself. For example, Ethernet at Layer 2 will work over copper or fiber at Layer 1. IP at Layer 3 can be transported over Ethernet or PPP at Layer 2. Figure 1-1 depicts the OSI seven-Layer OSI model.

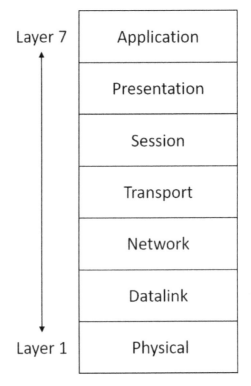

Figure 1-1, The OSI Seven Layer Model

Layer 1 - Physical

Layer 1 defines the physical characteristics of the transmission medium. This can be fiber optic cable, Cat 5, twisted pair telephone cable, X.21 and many more. One key point is that Layer 1 is oblivious to any higher layer and is not aware of any structure of the data frames transported over the medium.

Layer 2 - Datalink

The datalink layer provides for reliable communication between adjacent nodes. It is important to note that datalinks are only established between adjacent nodes and not end to end over a network. This concept is illustrated later. Layer 2 can correct errors over the link. The Point-to-Point Protocol (PPP), Ethernet, High Level Datalink Communications (HDLC) are all examples of Layer 2 datalink protocols. There are two sublayers within Layer 2. These are:

- Media Access Control (MAC) layer - responsible for controlling how devices in a network gain access to data and permission to transmit it
- Logical Link Control (LLC) layer - controls error checking and packet synchronization

Layer 3 – Network

The function of the network layer is to move data from source to destination. Layer 3 uses the concept of addresses to identify nodes on a network and protocols developed to perform this function are referred to as routed protocols. In addition, further protocols exist at Layer 3 to route traffic between nodes, and these are referred to as routing protocols.

The Internet Protocol (IP), Internetworking Packet Exchange (IPX) and The Datagram Delivery Protocol are all examples of routed protocols, while Open Shortest Path First (OSPF) and Routing Information Protocol (RIP) are examples of routing protocols.

Layer 4 – Transport

The transport layer is a host to host function. In other words, communication is established between the transmitting and receiving nodes and not the intermediate network. This layer is responsible for QoS functions, reliable data transfer and flow control.

The Transmission Control Protocol (TCP), is an example of a Layer 4 protocol.

Layer 5 – Session

The session layer is all about control connection between source and destination nodes. It involves the establishment and tear down of connections. Modes of transmission such as full or half duplex will be taken care of by this layer. As network engineers, we tend not to get involved in these higher layers as they are embedded in the applications.

Layer 6 – Presentation

This is one of the most esoteric layers. In short, the presentation layer provides a translation function between the application layer and the session layer. It may be that the application layer data for network transmission needs to be reformatted. One potential application may be encryption. This would be a function of the presentation layer.

Layer 7 – Application

It is important to note that the application layer is not the application itself. These software programs fall outside the scope of the OSI seven layer model. The application layer refers to the elements of a software application that controls the communication over a network. It interacts with the application and the presentation layer. Examples of application layer functions are Hypertext Transfer Protocol (HTTP), Simple Mail Transfer Protocol (SMTP) and File Transfer Protocol (FTP).

The OSI seven layer model is a generic model and over the years, manufacturers have developed technologies to deliver network services that align with the model. Many of these technologies are now redundant, but the prevalent implementation of the OSI model is based on TCP/IP. Figure 1-2 shows how TCP/IP is mapped to the OSI model.

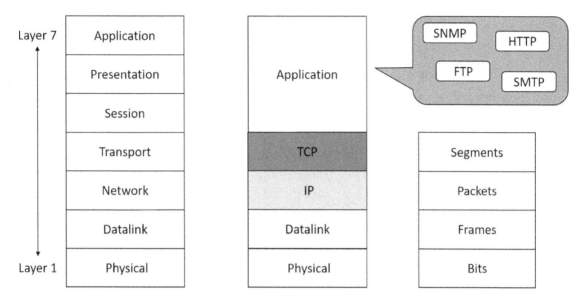

Figure 1-2, TCP/IP Mapped to the OSI Model

The Internet Protocol or IP sits at Layer 3 and TCP sits at Layer 4. The application may be familiar to the non-network savvy user. HTTP is the fundamental technology used to browse the Web. FTP is used to transfer files between network end points. SMTP is used for email. There are many more applications that run over TCP/IP. More about TCP/IP later.

The Internet Protocol

The Internet Protocol or IP resides at Layer 3 of the OSI stack. Layer 3 defines network addresses or locations. In principle, a network address is unique and just like a postal address, is used to route traffic from source to destination.

IP is practically the only Layer 3 protocol used today. There are alternatives such as IPX and Datagram Delivery Protocol, which were more common than IP in the late 1980s and early 1990s as they were a commercial offering bundled with operating systems, but they were supplanted by IP, which came to prominence with the growth of the Internet. IP is an open standard and so was a good choice for the Internet being free of commercial licensing.

IP version 4 is the most widely used version of IP, but IP version 6 will ultimately supersede IPv4 in the public network domain. IPv4 was originally defined in RFC 791 back in September 1981. It has since been updated in subsequent RFCs, but RFC 791 is the fundamental definition.

IPv4 has a complex header structure that can vary in size from 20 bytes to 60 bytes. The structure of this header is covered in chapter 4, so I make no reference to it here. A variable size header is problematic when delivering QoS, as it adds another variable factor making the IP flows indeterministic. It has many control features that would be useful for old, slow and unreliable transmission media used at the time but would be redundant now with today's reliable transmission media. It also has scalability issues as the address pool is limited by the 32 bits used for IPv4 addresses.

IPv6 remedies all these issues and the IPv6 header is also covered in chapter 4.

IP Version 4 Addressing

It is important understand the IP version 4 address format and meaning. An IP address defines a location on the network. That location could be a desktop computer, a printer or a server. In fact, it could be any endpoint we need to pass data to or retrieve data from. In simplistic terms, the IP address needs to be unique within the network, although there are technologies that allow duplication of IP addresses, mainly for reasons on scalability.

The IP version address is made up of a 32-bit binary number. Figure 1-3 is an example of an IP address in binary format.

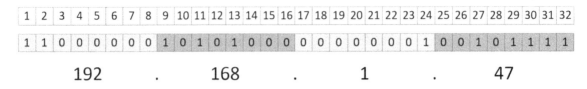

Figure 1-3, An Example of an IP Version 4 Address

A 32-bit address space will only allow us a total 4,294,967,296 (2^{32}) addresses. This is a limitation, given that every network device needs an IP address, and as a result, IPv4 address space is becoming exhausted. There are technologies available to increase scalability, but ultimately there is a real need to move to IPv6. There are new technologies, such as 5G, enabling the expansion of the Internet of Things. These new technologies drive increased demand for IP addresses for machine to machine communications.

Coming back to the example IP address in figure 1-3, a sequence of 32 binary numbers is not human friendly to work with. As a result, we tend to split the IP address into 8-bit segments and convert the 8-bit segment to a decimal number. Each decimal number is then separated by a dot. This is referred to decimal-dot notation. In our example, the 32-bit IP address can be expressed a 192.168.1.47.

The IP Version 4 Address Classes

We need to dig a little deeper into IP addressing to understand it fully. IP addresses each must have a portion that identifies the network and a portion that defines the host (the host being the device on that network). Historically, IPv4 addresses fell within one of five classes. The class defined the network host boundary. In 'Classful' terms, our example IP address would be a class C address. The network and host portion are shown in figure 1-4.

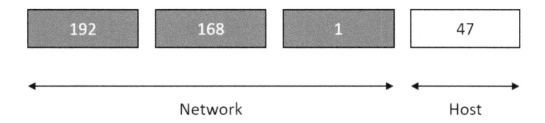

Figure 1-4, A Class C Address Showing the Network and Host Portions

The host portion in our example would have 8 bits. This means there can be up to 256 hosts in this network. However, 0 and 256 have special meaning. Zero is termed a 'wire address' and is used to identify the network segment. 256 would be set aside for broadcast traffic. Therefore, there are 254 useable addresses.

If a network has 6 workstations, each with a host address, and class C addressing is assigned to that network, then only 6 addresses would be needed. The remaining 248 would be set aside for expansion or simply wasted. Classful addressing is wasteful, and given the scalability constraints of IPv4, a more efficient IPv4 addressing methodology was needed, which led to the invention of the subnet mask.

The IPv4 Subnetting

The concept of IP address subnetting was introduced to provide a solution that would lead to increased efficiency when designing IP address schemes. What we may wish to avoid is allocating 254 hosts addresses to a network when a class C network is used for a smaller network of, say, 52 hosts. Figure 1-5 illustrates the concept of a subnet and subnet mask.

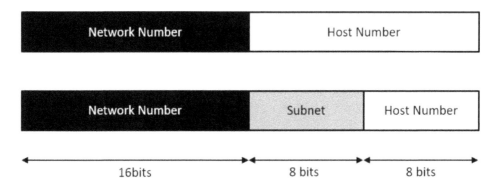

Figure 1-5, The IP Subnet Concept

The concept is quite simple. We can take a classful network and simply allocate some of the hosts bits to a 'subnetwork'. This reduces the number of host bits allocated to the host portion and increases the total amount of networks that can be address. In figure 1-5, a class B address is allocated to the network. In a class B network, 16 bits are assigned to the network number and 16 bits to the host. This would mean that each classful network would be able to address 65534 hosts. We could allocate 8 bits of the host portion to a subnet. This means we can support 256 subnets each with 8 bits allocated to the host portion. 8 bits equates to 254 hosts.

Let's look at a more specific example. In figure 1-6, we have a class B IP address of 172.16.1.47.

1	2	3	4	5	6	7	8	9	10	11	12	13	14	15	16	17	18	19	20	21	22	23	24	25	26	27	28	29	30	31	32	
1	0	1	0	1	1	0	0	0	0	0	1	0	0	0	0	0	0	0	0	0	0	0	1	0	0	1	0	1	1	1	1	IP Address
1	1	1	1	1	1	1	1	1	1	1	1	1	1	1	1	1	1	1	1	0	0	0	0	0	0	0	0	0	0	0	0	Subnet Mask

255 . 255 . 240 . 0

Figure 1-6, An IP Address Subnetting Example

There are 16 bits assigned to the network and 16 bits assigned to the host portion. We plan to assign 4 bits of the host portion to subnetworks leaving 12 bits for the host portion. 4 bits would give us 16 subnetworks. Each subnetwork will support up to 4094 hosts.

We need to identify what subnetwork our IP address belongs to and we achieve this by defining a subnetwork mask and assigning it to the IP address. A subnetwork mask is simply a 32-bit number with the bits in the network and subnetwork portions having value 1 and the bits in the host portion having value 0. In our example, the subnet mask in decimal-dot notation is 255.255.240.0. When using the IP address for a host, we need to assign both the IP address and the subnet mask, so the host understands what subnet it belongs to. For example, 172.16.1.47 255.255.240.0.

Subnetting is important so it is worth looking at another example. In this example, we wish to create a subnet that supports at least 34 hosts. We will assign a class C network for the task. The Class C network is 192.168.1.0. The ideal subnet will be just large enough to support 34 hosts and will provide enough spare host IP addresses for some expansion. The classful network portion will use 24 bits, so the question is what extra bits are needed for the subnet. A subnet of 3 bits will leave 5 host bits and so is only able to support 30 hosts, which would make it too small. Setting aside 2 bits for the subnet, however, will mean that we can provide 4 subnets with each subnet supporting 62 hosts. For our example the subnet mask will be 255.255.255.192 and it will meet our needs to support 34 hosts.

IP subnetting is important and does need some practice to fully understand. Guidance for further reading is provided at the end of this chapter.

Classless Interdomain Routing

Classless Interdomain Routing or CIDR, was introduced to provide more flexibility when subnetting IPv4 addresses and is widely used today. If you understand IP subnetting, then understanding CIDR is just a small step up. The notion of classful IP networks and subnets is replaced with a variable length subnet mask.

CIDR does introduce some concepts that are beyond the scope of this chapter, such as IP Super-netting, which allows IP routing tables in IP routers to be minimized. CIDR also provides the most efficient way of allocating IP addresses, thereby reducing wastage.

The subnet mask in CIDR is replaced with a Variable Length Subnet Mask (VLSM). In notational terms, it is the number of bits set to 1 in the mask. The IP address is appended with this number prefixed by a '/' symbol. For example, 192.168.2.54 255.255.255.0 is expressed as 192.168.2.54/24 and 172.16.47.1 255.255.240.0 is expressed as 172.16.47.1/20.

IP Version 6

The limitations of IPv4 were well understood by the mid 1990s. The complexities built into the IPv4 header were no longer needed as transmission media became much more reliable. In 1998, IPv6 was defined in RFC 2460. The IPv6 header is explained in chapter 4, so there is no need to cover it again here. The key point to remember about IPv6 is that the IP address field is 128bits in length. This means there are 340,282,366,920,938,463,463,374,607,431,768,211,456 IPv6 addresses. Like IPv4 addresses, IPv6 addresses are a string of 128 binary bits. We tend to express IPv6 addresses in groups of 4 hexadecimal numbers each separated by a colon. An example of which is below:

2001:cdba:0000:0000:0000:0000:3257:9652

There are ways to shorten this notation, but again that is beyond the scope of this chapter and is instead a topic for further reading.

Routing Protocols

IP is a protocol that operates at Layer 3 of the OSI stack. Layer 3 protocols identify a location on a network. To get traffic from one location to another, we need to implement a way to build a map of the network so that traffic knows how to get from the source location to the destination. This is the purpose of routing protocols.

Routing protocols fall into two basic types. These are Distance Vector and Link State routing protocols. There are also hybrid protocols, but these are beyond the scope of this chapter and in fact are becoming less important is modern networks.

Distance Vector Routing Protocols

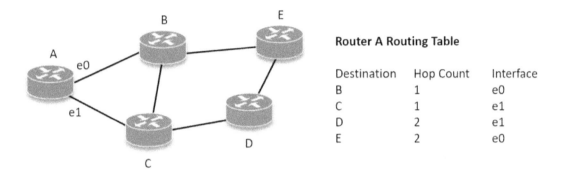

Router A Routing Table

Destination	Hop Count	Interface
B	1	e0
C	1	e1
D	2	e1
E	2	e0

Figure 1-7, The Distance Vector Concept

Distance Vector Routing Protocols are amongst the oldest routing protocols. The only one of note for modern networks is the Routing Information Protocol or RIP. Distance Vector protocols are based on the Bellman–Ford algorithm and the Ford–Fulkerson algorithms. These have their origins in the mid to late 1950s, but RIPv1 not standardized until 1988. The principles of Distance Vector routing are quite simple. Any destination has a distance from the source and a vector. The distance is based on the number of router hops in the path to the destination and the vector is the interface out of which the traffic will travel. Figure 1-7 illustrates this concept.

If traffic needs to get from Router A to Router E via the shortest route, then that route will be via Router B. The shortest route being 2 hops. The vector will be via interface e0. The principles of Distance Vector routing are as simple as that. There are some advantages and disadvantages of Distance Vector routing. One advantage is that it is simple to implement. It takes relatively little processing power. There are several disadvantages. The notion of a hop count bears no relationship to the actual bandwidth of the link. In figure 1-7, the links connecting Router A to Router B and router B to Router E may be very low in bandwidth compared to the other links. A Distance Vector routing protocol will always send traffic via the route with the lowest hop count even if the other routes have much higher bandwidth and are far more efficient. The other main disadvantage of RIP is that it sends its entire routing table periodically, about every 30 seconds. This means it is slow to converge should a failure occur as outages do not generate a triggered update. This update can also generate large amounts of traffic should the network contains many routers, so in general, RIP and Distance Vector routing protocols do not scale well. There are improvements available to RIP to helps address these issues, but these are beyond the scope of this chapter. Link State Routing Protocols are a better solution for large networks.

Link State Routing Protocols

Large modern networks will deploy a Link State protocol for routing. Link State protocols address all the limitations of Distance Vector protocols at the expense of needing greater processing resources. However, this is not an issue in modern network.

Link State protocols form what is termed 'neighbor relationships' with the routers they connect to. A router will then monitor the state of their neighbor relationship to assess whether they are up or down. They then periodically transmit their link state relationship to all routers in the network. This way, all routers can gather information about the entire network topology and the state of links within the network. If a link state changes the routers that are connected to that link can transmit this information immediately via a 'triggered update'. This leads to faster convergence compared to Distance Vector protocols that tend to periodically distribute their entire routing table.

Holding a current 'picture' of the entire network topology only provides a logical map of the network. This is akin to a road map that shows all routes to a destination. Like a driver with a road map, the router will then use this topology information to find the best route to the destination. Link State protocols use the Shortest Path First algorithm to find the best path. The shortest path first algorithm is based on Dijkstra's algorithm first proposed in the mid 1950s. The links in a Link State protocol are assigned a path cost. The path cost can factor in the bandwidth of a link so a high capability Gigabit Ethernet links can be given preference over a 2Mbps leased line. The algorithm then calculates the best path using the least cost rather than the lowest number of hops. Figure 1-8 illustrates the concept.

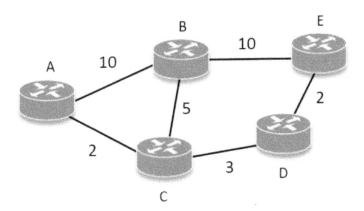

Figure 1-8, The Shortest Path First Algorithm

In figure 1-8, the shortest path from Router A to Router E will via Router C as the total path cost is 2+3+2=7. This path is 3 hops but has the lowest path cost. The path via Router B only has 2 hops, but the total path cost is 20.

There are two noteworthy modern link State Routing protocols. Open Shortest Path First version 2 or OSPFv2 is the most widely deployed. This protocol is only able to route IP traffic and no other Layer 3 protocols. Furthermore, OSPFv2 is only able to route IPv4. OSPF version 3 is needed to route IPv6, but OSPFv3 cannot route IP version 4. This leads to some interesting technical challenges.

Intermediate System to Intermediate System or IS-IS can route multiple Layer 3 protocols including IPv4 and IPv6. It is still popular amongst carrier providers for this reason, but for most enterprises OSPF is the protocol of choice.

Interior and Exterior Routing Protocols

RIP, OSPF and IS-IS are considered Interior Gateway Protocols or IGPs. They are designed to be administered by one entity within their network. An administrative entity can be an enterprise or carrier organization. In networking terms these protocols will reside within a single Autonomous System (AS).

However, we need to consider the Internet. The internet is made up of the networks of multiple organizations or multiple Autonomous Systems. We use Exterior Gateway Protocols or EGPs to route between Autonomous Systems.

The Border Gateway Protocol (BGP) is the only EGP that is used today. BGP can be considered as a derivate of a Distance Vector protocol. In strict terms it is a 'Path Vector' protocol. The path to a destination is made up of a string of the Autonomous Systems the packet must traverse to reach its destination. The vector is the exit interface. Autonomous Systems are identified by a AS unique number.

Routing across the Internet bears much responsibility and BGP provides a complex set of attributes and policy-based features that allow fine tuning of traffic flow. BGP has no automatic discovery mechanism and so peer relationships between BGP routers must be set up manually. For this reason, public IP addresses, AS numbers and other Internet Protocol resources are regulated by The Internet Assigned Numbers Authority (https://www.iana.org/).

Guidance for further reading into BGP is provided at the end if this chapter.

Ethernet

Having briefly discussed Layer 3 routing, we need to look closer at Layer 2 of the OSI stack. Ethernet is becoming the dominant connectivity medium in both the Local Area Network (LAN) and the Wide Area Network (WAN). There are services that run at Layer 2 only and require QoS treatment for different traffic types. Therefore, having a basic understanding of Ethernet technology is essential.

Ethernet has its origins as a networking infrastructure technology for the Local Area Network. It was first standardized in 1983 as IEEE 802.3. It is fast becoming the transmission media of choice for Service Providers too. This is primarily because it is cheap, scalable and works over many different physical media such as copper cabling and fiber optics. Ethernet does have its limitations, but its low cost and ubiquitous nature has meant it has largely displaced better engineered, but much more expensive, technologies such as PDH and SDH.

The basic Ethernet frame does not have any means to carry Class of Service (CoS) information. However, enhancements in the IEEE 802.1Q gave Ethernet this capability. These are covered in chapter 4.

Basic Ethernet has a simple frame structure and is shown in figure 1-9.

6 bytes	6 bytes	2 bytes	Up to 1500 bytes	4 bytes
DA	SA	Len/ type	Data	FCS

Standard Ethernet Frame

DA: Destination MAC address
SA: Source MAC address
Len/type: Frame length or Ethertype
Data: The user data
FCS: Frame Check Sequence

Figure 1-9, The Basic Ethernet Frame

The first field in the frame is the address of the destination. The second field is the source address, i.e. the address of where the frame came from. These fields are swapped for return the traffic. The next field provides an indication of the protocol being carried in the payload. For instance, 0800 HEX signifies that IP is being carried. We then have a variable length payload. A Cyclic Redundancy Check (termed Frame Check Sequence) completes the frame. The purpose of the FCS is to detect errors in the frame.

The address format is significant and deserves some attention. The source and destination address in an Ethernet frame are MAC addresses or Media Access Control addresses. MAC addresses are 48 bits in length. 24 bits are assigned to a manufacturer and referred to as the Organizationally Unique Identifier (OUI). The remaining bits are allocated by the manufacturer and are referred to as Network Interface Controller (NIC) Specific. The key thing is that MAC addresses are meant to be globally unique and each MAC address is 'burnt in' at the hardware level. Every Ethernet interface has a MAC address burnt into the electronics. The format of a MAC address is shown in figure 1-10.

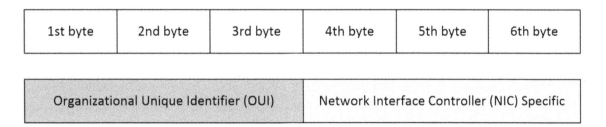

Figure 1-10, The MAC Address Format

Multi-Protocol Label Switching

Figure 1-11 is an illustration of what happens with traditional Layer 3 routing in a network with respect to the OSI stack.

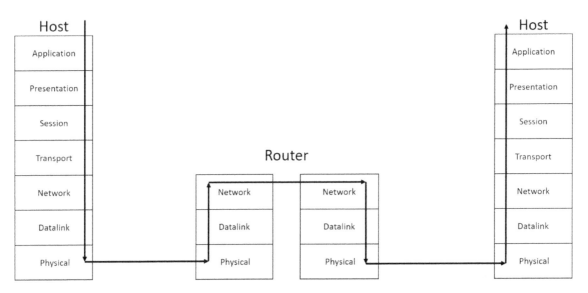

Figure 1-11, Layer 3 Routing and the OSI Stack

When packets enter a router, the Layer 2 frame header is stripped, and what is left is sent up to Layer 3. Layer 3 performs a look up against the routing table and the packet is sent down to Layer 2 where is it re-framed and sent to the egress interface. This happens for every packet on every router. This requires a lot of processing power and for large networks, it may overload the router's processor and it is inefficient. It would be more efficient if the router could perform some type of Layer 2 lookup and bypass the Layer 3. Carriers deploy Multi-Protocol Label Switching or MPLS to do this job.

The MPLS frame components are described in chapter 4 and so are not covered here. Furthermore, how MPLS is used to deliver QoS is covered in detail in chapter 10, Traffic Engineering. However, there is a significant amount of terminology associated with MPLS that we need to review to better understand the technology.

Figure 1-12 illustrates a basic MPLS network and is used to help explain the key terminology.

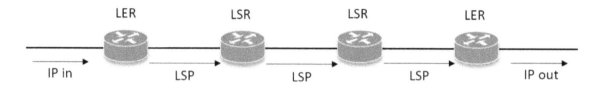

Figure 1-12, A basic MPLS Network

Label Edge Router (LER)

Label Edge Routers reside at the edge of the MPLS domain and push an MPLS label onto the incoming packets and pop the label for outgoing packets.

Label Switch Router (LSR)

Label Switches Routers reside within the MPLS domain and swap the label of the incoming packet with a new label before sending it along its path. LSRs do not perform IP lookup, but only forward packets based on the MPLS label.

Label Switched Path (LSP)

This is the path that a MPLS headed frame takes from source to destination. LSPs are unidirectional and as such a packet may take a different path from source to detention compared to destination to source.

MPLS Operation

Figure 1-13 helps explain MPLS operation.

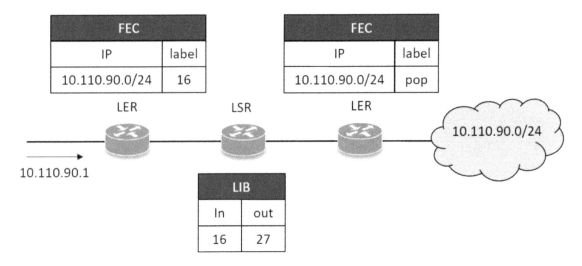

Figure 1-13, MPLS Operation

At the edge of the MPLS network, packets enter the LER. Here, the LER has a table referred to as the Forwarding Equivalence Class (FEC). Destination IP addresses in the IP header are matched to a MPLS label value. In this example, the destination IP network is 10.110.90.0/24 and the label value is 16. An MPLS header or shim is pushed onto the packet and the resultant MPLS frame is forwarded out of the required interface. The MPLS frame will arrive at an LSR. The LSR has a Label Information Base (LIB). It is simply a case of looking at the incoming label value and swapping that with an outgoing label value and forwarding the MPLS on its way. In this example, 16 is swapped with 27. At the egress LER, the MPLS label is popped and the IP packet forwarded on using normal IP lookup rules.

Switches and Routers

We have spent quite some time introducing Layer 2 and Layer 3 technologies without understanding the equipment needed to support these technologies. At a basic level, it is essential to gain a fundamental understanding of switches and routers.

Generally, switches are used to connect hosts (e.g. computers, printer and servers) within a Local Area Network (LAN). They operate at Layer 2 and most commonly nowadays are Ethernet based. They may be small, having a few physical Ethernet ports, or may be much larger, having many hundreds of ports. Devices connected to the network will also have Ethernet ports and these are connected directly to the switch using copper RJ45 cabling. Switched networks are easy to set up and there may be no configuration needed on the switch itself. Figure 1-14 illustrates this concept.

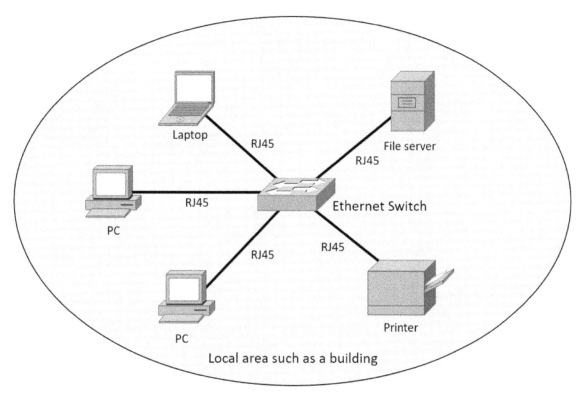

Figure 1-14, A Switched Network

Routers on the other hand, are used to connect networks together. They operate at Layer 3 of the OSI stack. Routers provide a means for data to be forwarded to other networks. At the basic level a network will have a single router that is often called the gateway. As the term implies, all data that is destined for a different network is passed to this router. The data is then passed to the destination via a network of routers running routing protocols. Figure 1-15 illustrates this concept.

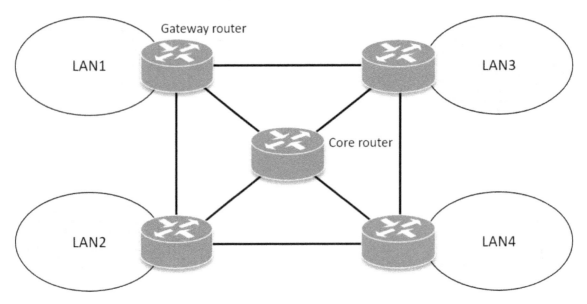

Figure 1-15, A Routed Network

Further Reading

This chapter is only intended to guide those who are new to networking. It introduces the reader to the fundamental technologies needed to learn about the more complex topics such as QoS in Packet Switched networks. Further reading and practice will be needed to develop a deeper and more complete understanding to the subject. Therefore, the following provides some direction and focus areas for further study. There is much information freely available on the Internet, so specific references are not included while key areas for study are highlighted.

- Learn about the role of the Transmission Control Protocol (TCP) and the User Datagram Protocol (UDP) has in Layer 4 of the OSI and their relationship to IP
- Learn about difference between Public and Private IP address space, particularly RFC 1918
- Practice IP subnetting to work out network range, i.e. the network number, broadcast address and what are host IPs. There are online CIDR calculators that will help

- Learn about the difference IPv6 address types of unicast, multicast and anycast. Also gain an understanding of how to shorten IPv6 address notation
- Dig deeper into how RIP, OSPF and BGP operate
- Learn about the Label Distribution Protocol (LDP) in relation to MPLS
- Investigate PDH, SDH and SONET technologies to gain a basic understanding of how they work
- Look at the web to gain a better understanding of the switching and routing equipment available from manufacturers such as Cisco, Juniper, Netgear and others

Chapter 2: Historical Initiatives

We can trace the earliest practical work to develop computer-based networks back to the mid to late 1960s. These early networks were designed to transfer data between mainframe computers to facilitate time sharing, as processing power was a scarce and expensive resource. The Pentagon's Advanced Research Projects Agency Network (or Arpanet) is the most noteworthy of these projects. Arpanet's achievement was to realize the concept of packet switching. Despite its successes, Arpanet can be judged a failure to some degree on the basis that the numerous computers involved used different operating systems, versions and programs and it therefore proved very difficult to interwork with someone else's computer. However, significant developments were made with Arpanet, which led directly to the creation of the first Internet. These developments included email, packet switching implementations, and development of the (Transport Control Protocol - Internet Protocol) or TCP/IP.

Arpanet was all about retrieving and processing data at a remote location. Never, at any stage, was their thought of using the same network for voice or video communications given any serious attention. The question of QoS need not be considered. Would it matter if the data was received in 2 seconds, 10 seconds or 5 minutes? Would it matter if some data was lost on its way? TCP would detect those losses and instruct the sender to resend it. Clearly the performance parameters that can be applied to the transfer of data across a network cannot be applied the transfer of voice across a network. Aside from that, the development of digital voice networks was ongoing separately. These programs led to the development of digital circuit switching technology. Whereas getting computers the talk to each other was viewed as an academic pastime, there was real money to be made in telephony, so it is little wonder that circuit switching digital networks were implemented well in advance of any data networks, either in the local area or wide area environments.

Circuit Switching and Packet Switching

Clearly when you want to transport voice over a digital network QoS must be an absolute given. You would expect your call to get through to the other line. You would expect the line to be clear of noise and the speech not to break up or be garbled. Circuit switching networks where built fundamentally to transport voice traffic. The network establishes a fixed bandwidth circuit between nodes and terminals before the users may communicate. These resources are maintained throughout the duration of the call. This ensures that the user experiences the QoS they expect. Each circuit cannot be used by other callers until the circuit is released and a new connection is set up. Figure 2-1 illustrates the concept.

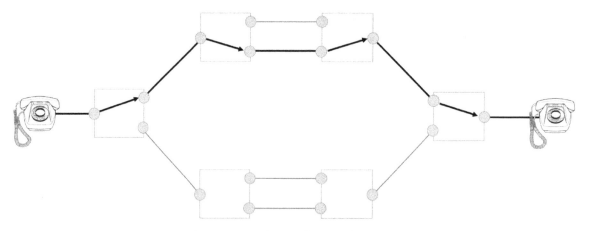

Figure 2-1, Circuit Switched Concept

If we stay with the telephony example, the earliest systems simply connected physical copper lines together at a manned exchange. As systems advanced, it was possible to multiplex multiple lines onto a single line, but the same principle still applies - that a dedicated circuit was set aside for the call. Work in the early 1970s led to the first digital telephone networks based on the Plesiochronous Digital Hierarchy (PDH). Demands for greater capacity and operational simplicity led to the development of Synchronous Digital Hierarchy (SDH) and Synchronous Optical Networking (SONET). The fundamental building block for all these technologies was the bandwidth used by a single digitized telephone call. As such the same circuit switching resource reservation concepts applied to these technologies.

In a packet switching network, as shown in Figure 2-2, data in the form of packets is routed between nodes using shared data links. Packets are discrete blocks of data and unlike voice traffic, data packets are of variable length. They can also be queued or buffered as no bandwidth (or connection) is reserved up front. This leads to variable delays in transmission and potential packet loss if buffers get full. Furthermore, there is no guarantee that all packets from one source will take the same route over a network to a destination.

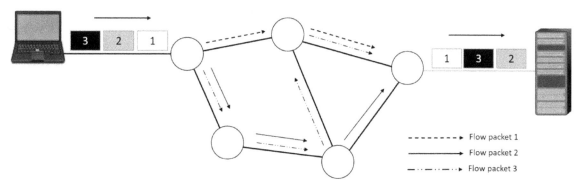

Figure 2-2, Packet Switched Concept

So, we have two distinct engineering solutions. One for the transport of voice and one for the transport of data. Historically, voice and data would be transported over two separate infrastructures using what can be described as 'opposing' technologies. The key features are summarized in table 2-1.

Voice Transport	Data Transport
Connection oriented	Connectionless
Fixed data lengths	Variable data lengths
Predicable delay	Variable delay
No retransmission for data loss	Retransmission for data loss

Table 2-1, A Comparison between Voice Transport and Data Transport

Therefore, there were separate networks for voice and data, using their own technologies specifically engineered to meet the needs of that traffic type. This status quo remained until the mid-1990s. Throughout the 1990s we saw what only can be described as exponential growth in the processing power of personal computers. This placed demands on network capacity as file sizes increased accordingly and advancements were made in data types such as graphics and digital video. PDH and SDH networks, being primarily designed to transport voice, were able to transfer computer data. Scaling of these carrier class technologies to higher bandwidths was achieved, but at significant financial cost. This cost was too much to bear for many enterprises, so it comes as little wonder that enterprise class technologies for data networks became more significant. The key technology of the enterprise was Ethernet. Ethernet proved to be very low cost, scalable and easy to implement and support and in the mid to late 1990s, was scaled to beyond what was required for data transfer. Adding extra capacity to an Ethernet network was cheap, and Ethernet was dominant in the local area, so it was clear that the enterprise sector would soon ask the question 'why do we need separate networks for voice and data'? The economics could not be questioned and 'network convergence', as it is called, was inevitable - it was only a matter of time. The problem was that this data networking technology exhibited all the data networking characteristics highlighted in table 2-1. So, if voice where to be transported over a converged network, additional technologies would have to be engineered to deliver the correct QoS to the different traffic types.

Over the years, there have been numerous definitions given to the term Quality of Service. A general definition that applies today is: QoS refers to a broad collection of networking technologies and techniques. The goal of QoS is to provide guarantees on the ability of a network to deliver predictable results.

Some of the earliest technologies were specifically designed to run over PDH and SDH networks. These technologies are on the decline today as these networks are replaced by Ethernet networks. However, some of the legacy QoS technologies have been adopted by the Metro Ethernet Forum and adapted for Ethernet environments. Consequently, these technologies were built into modern Carrier Ethernet devices and two noteworthy network transport mechanisms that merit some attention are Asynchronous Transfer Mode (ATM) and Frame Relay. The QoS technologies from these two were adapted for use in Carrier Ethernet networks.

Frame Relay

There is an underlying principle that applies to all networks with respect to QoS. If there is more bandwidth available on a network link than the sum of the bandwidths of all the traffic flows on that link, then there is no need to implement QoS. There is enough capacity on the link to guarantee that all traffic will leave that node. Only if there is more demand for bandwidth than what is available on that link will there be a need to prioritize traffic and apply QoS. The Frame Relay forum, as it was at the time, developed QoS mechanisms for operation within Frame Relay.

Implementation Agreements for Frame Relay began to immerge in 1994. Importantly, it is a circuit switching technology that was designed to run over PDH networks. It was designed to transport voice and data over the same physical link. Frame Relay overlays 'virtual circuits' over the PDH circuit to logically partition the single PDH network into multiple virtually private networks. Most of these virtual circuits where implemented in the form of Permanent Virtual Circuits (PVCs). The use of a PVC meant a permanent connection between its source and destination. In order to reserve the necessary bandwidth within a PVC, the concept of a Committed Information Rate (CIR) was engineered into the Frame Relay. The CIR is what a service provider will guarantee, in terms of bandwidth, for that PVC. The CIR would be measured in Kilobits per second.

A typical traditional PDH voice flow would have a constant bit rate of 64Kbps and this bandwidth is still used even if there is silence on the call. A typical computer data flow, such as a file transfer does not exhibit such characteristics. Computer data flows are typically asynchronous. A request for a file is a simple short message. The file that is returned may be very large in comparison. If there is no communication between computers then, unlike for silence in a voice call, no bandwidth is used. Computer related data transfers are said to be 'bursty' in nature. Frame Relay also introduced another important concept - the Excess Information Rate (EIR). The EIR is the amount of data that a flow can use over and above the CIR if there is unused bandwidth on the link. The EIR may be set to the line rate of the network link. To ensure that all guaranteed traffic reaches its destination without loss, the sum of the CIRs on a link should not exceed the bandwidth of the link. If the EIR of any flow is set to the line rate, any flow can then use spare capacity if it is available, but must submit to any flow that may need to use that bandwidth to meet its CIR. This clearly leads to a concept of fairness, such that a bandwidth greedy file transfer cannot starve a voice call, yet at the same time ensures the greatest link efficiency with no wasted bandwidth. The concepts of CIR and EIR were very important developments. Although Frame Relay is on the decline and heading toward end of life as a commercially viable offering, the exact same CIR and EIR concepts have been embraced by the Metro Ethernet Forum and are implemented across all Metro Ethernet Forum (MEF) compliant Carrier Ethernet devices.

Asynchronous Transfer Mode (ATM)

Frame Relay was a very significant protocol. However, it suffered from three significant drawbacks that forced network developers to look for a new solution. Frame Relay was primarily designed to run over PDH networks with access bandwidths up to 45Mbps. Voice capacity alone in the late 1980s meant that network capacity had to scale beyond the 45Mbps limits of PDH. SONET and SDH networks were being introduced in the early 1990s. These early networks were designed to scale from 155Mbps up to 622Mbps. Modern SDH and SONET networks scale to 10Gbps and even 40Gbps. The hierarchical nature of SONET and SDH means that PDH tributaries can be connected to these networks.

Frames of data within Frame Relay networks (akin to packets within IP networks) are of variable length. This introduced the concept of 'jitter' for voice traffic. Jitter can be defined as the variation in delay that a traffic flow suffers over a network. Jitter is not necessarily a significant factor in today's high-speed networks. However, for low speed access, up to 2Mbps, jitter becomes significant and affects voice quality.

Voice frames are small, say 80 bytes and may require 64Kbps of bandwidth. Consider a situation where just voice is running over a 256Kbps link. Setting all other factors aside, the voice frames should have consistent delay over the network. In this simplified example, the delay variation, or jitter, is zero.

The same Frame Relay PVC is now used to transport a data flow as well as the voice. The data flow's frames are 1500 bytes in length. Consider a situation where a data frame is transmitted in between two voice frames. The time taken to transmit the data frame across the link is:

$T = |(1500 \text{x} 8)/256000|$ seconds

T = 0.047 seconds

This will introduce a delay of 0.047 seconds in between the voice frames, and this delay is enough to affect the quality of the voice to the human ear. In fact, the accepted service level for jitter in voice communications is less than 0.035 seconds or 35ms.

256Kbps may seem like a low bandwidth by today's standards. However, in the late 1990s a 256Kbps link would have been expensive for any enterprise organization. Links of 64Kbps to 512Kbps were common, with 1MBps and 2Mbps links being considered high end for the enterprise.

The scene was set for Asynchronous Transfer Mode (ATM) to become dominant as a network technology for network convergence and ATM standards started to emerge from 1995. ATM was designed to work over PDH and SDH networks for greater scalability compared to Frame Relay. The unique point of ATM was that all data was split into small, constant sizes cells of 53 bytes; 48 bytes of payload and 5 bytes of header information. Like Frame Relay, ATM is a circuit switching technology that utilizes PVCs.

Aside from increased scalability, what attracted service providers to ATM was the fact that all types of data are transmitted in these small cells. Cells of a voice flow could be inserted in between cells of a large data flow. This ensured that jitter was no longer an issue when low speed links were used. ATM had similar features to the CIR and EIR in Frame Relay. In fact, for the purposes of this book, the Sustainable Cell Rate (SCR) of ATM can be considered as having the same function and definition as the Committed Information Rate (CIR) of Frame Relay. Likewise, the Peak Cell Rate (PCR) of ATM is akin to the Excess Information Rate (EIR) of Frame Relay.

The idea of a truly converged network was well established by the time ATM was being standardized. As a result, support for specific traffic types was built into the technology. There are four basic traffic types amongst other variations. These basic types are:

- **Constant Bit Rate (CBR)**: you specify a Peak Cell Rate (PCR), which is constant. Voice would typically be a CBR flow
- **Variable Bit Rate (VBR)**: you specify an average or Sustainable Cell Rate (SCR), which can peak (using the PCR) at a certain level for a maximum interval before becoming problematic. Compressed video would fall into this category
- **Available Bit Rate (ABR)**: you specify a minimum guaranteed rate. Business critical data would be suitable for this traffic type

- **Unspecified Bit Rate (UBR)**: traffic is allocated all remaining transmission capacity. Best efforts traffic and non-critical data would normally be UBR traffic

From a QoS perspective, ATM addresses all the issues. Many will argue that from a technology perspective, ATM will never be bettered and it is certainly a robust technology. However, if that is indeed the case, why has it declined to point that it is obsolete?

In fact, there are several reasons for its decline. First, there are 5 bytes of header data for each cell. With only 48 bytes of data within each cell, there is a significant overhead with ATM and links can never run at more than 95% efficiency. Second, is the question of scalability. ATM in the mid 1990s was designed for a maximum speed of 622Mbps. Work to increase this to 2.5Gbps was not completed until 1999. 10Gbps ATM would not be standardized until 2003, which would prove to be too late for the demands placed on service providers by the now booming and fully commercial Internet. By the year 2000, service providers were demanding backbone link speeds of 10Gbps, so the technology was simply getting left behind. The third reason was complexity. It was first envisaged that ATM would propagate all the way to the desktop and would be present in the LAN and WAN. Ethernet had been around since the early 1980s, was well understood, and was very easy to implement and support. The technology was also very scalable and, crucially, very cheap. Fast Ethernet links of 100Mbps were around in the LAN when ATM was still in its early days. There was never a viable business case for ATM to displace the established Ethernet in the LAN and so complex and expensive routers were still needed. The final reason, therefore, is the cost associated with ATM. The level of engineering and the precise nature of the ATM components comes at a cost and this cost was too great for many service providers and too great for most enterprises. In fact, the enterprises were having to invest in expensive routers at the edge of their networks to interface between their Ethernet LANs and the ATM or Frame Relay WAN. The prime concern for the enterprise was to get data from a local LAN to the LAN of a remote site. They saw these expensive routers simply as expensive protocol converters.

It is no wonder, therefore, that enterprises placed pressure on Service Providers to introduce end to end Ethernet networks. This would mean that Service Providers would need to move to Packet Switching Networks and introduce all the deficiencies that these networks had when it came to delivering QoS. The following chapters go on to describe some of the industry initiatives to address the problems that packet switching brought to network convergence.

Chapter 3: Integrated Services

So far, we have looked briefly at QoS models adopted by the Circuit Switched technologies of ATM and Frame Relay. It is true to say that these technologies were used to transport Internet traffic. However, the Internet evolved from Arpanet during the 1980s and the Internet, like Arpanet, is based on packet switching technology. packet switching and circuit switching can be considered mutually exclusive, so the IP based Internet could only be 'overlaid' on top of ATM transport networks. The IP network was essentially another data application. The ATM element had to be provisioned and managed separately to the IP element. This is complex and expensive to deliver and manage, and as mentioned previously, ATM is also an expensive technology with significant scalability issues. There was a real need to develop QoS technologies that could be applied to native IP networks to overcome these limitations.

As the size of the Internet grew in the early 1990s, its commercial potential was beginning to be well understood - as too were the potential savings that could be made by offering business class data services over the Internet. The question of convergence over the Internet was being asked and developers started to look for solutions.

The Internet uses the Internet Protocol (IP) to identify nodes or end points on the networks, with each end point or node having a unique IP address. The Internet is made up of routers that hold the information required to enable the end points to communicate with one another. There was no provision in the early Internet for any QoS. Many networks were built in the form of meshes, and individual links could be of any bandwidth. The job of routers was only to get traffic from source to destination. If there was more than one route between sites, then there was no guarantee that any one specific route may be used and there was little to stop a 64Kbps link being used in preference to a 2Mbps link between two sites. This limitation could be overcome to some degree by using Link State routing protocols. Link State protocols such as IS-IS and OSPF have a cost assigned to individual links and the lower the cost, the more bandwidth that link has. The path with the lowest cost is preferred over higher cost paths. In the early 1990s, however, OSPF had not been standardized and Link State protocols required a lot of router processing and memory. With networks being relatively small and simple, Distance Vector protocols, such as RIP, were the norm in many networks. Distance Vector protocols simply look for the path with the lowest number of hops – meaning they could use a single 2Mbps link in preference to two 10Mbps links. It must be borne in mind that the function of routing protocols is to find a path – preferably the best available path - for data flow to get from source to destination. When there are multiple flows on that path, routing protocols do not have any mechanisms to ensure that high priority data has preference over low priority data should that path experience congestion.

The Integrated Services (IntServ) architecture was developed by the Internet Engineering Task Force (IETF) and released as 'RFC 1633' in 1994. It was motivated by the needs of real-time applications such as remote video, multimedia conferencing, visualization, and virtual reality. IntServ comprises seven major components and while, as an architectural model, IntServ is not used today, some of its components are used in the Differentiated Services (DiffServ) model, which is widely used to deliver QoS over modern IP based packet networks. The seven components are categorized as:

- **Resource Reservation**: An end to end signaling function to ensure a data flow has adequate resources through the network
- **Admission Control**: determines whether a new flow can be granted the requested QoS without impacting existing reservations
- **Policy Control**: is the user allowed to make reservations?
- **Classification**: recognize packets that need particular levels of QoS
- **Policing**: take action, including the possibly of dropping packets, when traffic does not conform to its specified characteristics
- **Queuing and Scheduling**: forward packets according to those QoS requests that have been granted
- **Packet Dropping**: Congestion Control mechanism to prevent TCP global synchronization

RFC 1633 is an overview document which sets the scene for further development. Rather than presenting tight functional specifications, RFC 1633 can be regarded as a framework document. Equipment manufacturers would interpret this framework in their own way and inevitably go down their own specific route when implementing IntServ on their own equipment. Either a consensus or further standardization was therefore required and this becomes apparent when we look at the IntServ architecture in more detail.

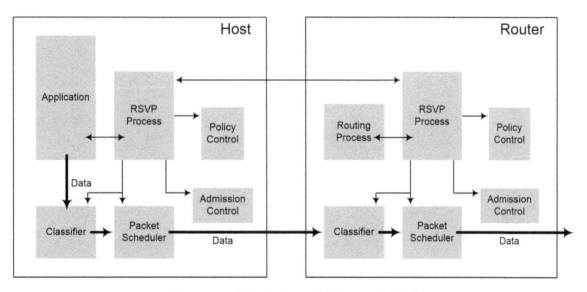

Figure 3-1, The IntServ Architectural Model

Figure 3-1 illustrates the IntServ architectural model. Two initial points to note are that resource reservations are unidirectional and since data will inevitably need to be returned to the sender, QoS for this flow will need to be set up separately. The second point is that IntServ is designed to be host to host (or application to application) and is not limited to the packet network elements alone, e.g. router to router. This is significant if you consider that a Service Provider will offer routing services, and so they may not want to hand off control to their customer's application for all resource reservation requests.

The Resource Reservation Protocol (RSVP)

IntServ relies on end to end signaling to ensure that QoS is possible throughout the network for a given flow. The principle of operation is that an application residing on a host knows what treatment its traffic needs for acceptable performance. Before any data transfer begins, the sender makes a request for resources from the network and this request for resources is either granted or denied. The Resource reSerVation Protocol (RSVP), as described in RFC 2205 was developed for this task. It is a signaling protocol only and does not take part in data transfer.

RSVP is unidirectional and Figure 3-2 illustrates the basic operation of RSVP.

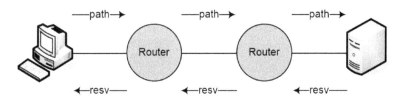

Figure 3-2, RSVP Message Flow

The sender sends out a resource request messages destined for the receiver. These messages are called 'path' messages. Each router in the path notes the contents of the path messages and holds this information in the form of a 'path state'. No reservation is made at this stage. Eventually, the 'path' message arrives at the receiver. The receiver then sends back a 'reservation' or 'resv' message along the path to the original sender. It is these 'resv' messages that reserve the network resources. When the sender receives the 'resv' message the data flow will begin. There are two modules required for RSVP to function. They answer two basic questions:

- Are there enough resources to make the reservation?
- Does the user have permission to make reservations?

Admission Control

This is a module associated with RSVP and answers the question: "are there sufficient resources to make the reservation?" All routers along a path must decide to set aside resources for a given flow or reject the request. The admission control function is the element within IntServ that tracks the path states. RSVP will consult the Admission Control function of a router to see if resources exist in response to a request.

Policy Control

This is the second module associated with RSVP and answers the question: "does the user have permission to make reservations?" Policy Control and Admission Control combine to apply some form of 'back pressure' on RSVP requests to prevent abuse by users, as ultimately RSVP will allow preferential treatment of some traffic.

The Classifier

Traffic flowing over the network needs to be identified so that it receives the appropriate treatment. Incoming packets are said to be classified. All packets of the same class get the same treatment from the Packet Scheduler - the IntServ Classifier performs this function.

A traffic class may be passed according to the contents of the IP header or some additional information (more details of packet classification techniques are provided in chapter 4). A class might correspond to a broad category of flows, e.g. all video flows or all flows attributable to a single organization. On the other hand, a class might hold only a single flow. IntServ also states that a class may only have local significance such that any router may apply a different class to a traffic flow.

The packet classification techniques developed for IntServ are still in used today in the DiffServ model. Packet classification is covered in more detail in chapter 4.

The Packet Scheduler

Packet scheduling or queuing involves re-ordering the packet at the output stage such that high priority packets are forwarded ahead of lower priority packets. RFC 1633 does not seek to dictate the actual scheme or schemes used, but it mentions schemes such as Strict Priority and Weighted Fair Queuing and alludes to more complex combined schemes. There is very little detail of how packet schedulers should work in RFC 1633. However, packet scheduling and queuing are important subjects and are covered in detail in chapter 5.

Packet Dropping

Packet Dropping is a congestion avoidance mechanism and the subject of packet dropping is discussed in RFC 1633, although no specific schemes are defined. RFC 1633 does, however, refer to independent work that was on-going around the mid 1990s. Congestion avoidance is discussed in chapter 6 (see WRED) and requires an overview of TCP behavior to understand the reasons why congestion avoidance is important. This, too, is covered in chapter 6.

Integrated Services as a Practical QoS Architecture

The reality is that IntServ is deficient in too many areas for it to be a practical solution for providing QoS over packet switching, specifically for large, IP based networks.

The definitions above contain nearly as much detail as is described in RFC 1633. As stressed earlier, the Integrated Service Architectural model is a framework and a set of definitions upon which further work would be needed if the model were to be realized. RSVP and Packet Dropping were ultimately well defined and well understood by equipment manufacturers and Service Providers alike. However, classification and packet scheduling require cooperation between equipment manufacturers and Service Providers if a consistent end to end QoS policy is to be implemented and all Service Providers have their own view as to how different service classes should be treated by their network. The Internet is made up of many IP networks with many separate and competing Service Providers. In this climate, getting the service providers to agree and cooperate to provide the user with an end to end QoS policy, is problematic at best. From the equipment manufacturers' perspective, the main area of difference is associated with packet scheduling. As will be discussed later, there are many schemes implemented that deliver different results. Although there is now some convergence and harmonization of these techniques, there are still differences that make a consistent end to end and multi-vendor QoS policy difficult.

There is one major technical reason that prevented large scale implementation of the IntServ model: scalability issues with RSVP. A path state would need to be maintained on every router for every flow that requires QoS. Given the sheer size of the Internet, this simply would not be possible and routers would cease to function as their CPUs became overloaded.

Finally, the actual setup of paths using RSVP implies that circuits are established. Therefore, IntServ implies packet switching technology can behave like circuit switching technology. The path of the RSVP messages implies all packets will take the same route from source to destination. In a stable and simple network this would most likely be true as routing protocols would choose single best path. The reality, however, is that any large IP based network (in particular the Internet), is not so stable. Links will fail or are administratively taken out of service for commercial or operational reasons. In addition, some routing protocols load balance over multiple paths where multiple routes exist. For each route change a new RSVP path must be signaled and existing paths must be refreshed to ensure they are still valid. This, too, adds to the burden on the network.

The reality is that for QoS to scale effectively, and to be widely deployed, RSVP should not be used. End to end resource reservation is simply not viable. The ideal technology would allow each router in a network to make individual judgments as to how packets should be treated based on a predefined service class. This approach eliminates both the need for advance signaling and the need to hold path states. The best elements of the Integrated Services Architecture would be taken forward and incorporated into the Differentiated Services Architectural Model (DiffServ). DiffServ is the most widely deployed QoS model today in both Enterprise and Service Provider IP networks.

Before examining the DiffServ model in more detail, it is important to understand that key elements of the Integrated Services Model are also used in DiffServ. These areas are packet classification, packet scheduling and congestion control (packet dropping). Therefore, it is worth exploring these areas in more detail to gain an understanding of the mechanisms available today.

Before moving on, it is also worth noting that the work on RSVP was not wasted. RSVP turned out to be the ideal signaling mechanism for Multi-Protocol Label Switching based Traffic Engineering (MPLS-TE). MPLS-TE is covered in detail in chapter 10.

Chapter 4: Packet Classification

It has long been recognized that data packets may need a mechanism to classify or differentiate themselves from other packets so that they can receive preferential treatment over a network. This book is not intended to provide an overview of networking principles, but the concept of network layering needs to be discussed to understand the context of specific packet classification mechanisms. It was clear from early attempts to network computers that different implementations, operating systems and applications would cause inter-working problems. The Open Systems Interconnection Basic Reference Model (OSI model) was developed as an attempt to simplify computer networking and provide the building blocks for a standards-based approach to computer network. The OSI model comprises seven layers, but only layers 1 through 4 have any relevance for us in the context of understanding QoS in packet networks.

Today, we only need focus on Ethernet and the Internet Protocol (IP). These are two standards that reside in the first three layers of the OSI model and Figure 4-1 shows the layers of the OSI model that IP and Ethernet relate to. It is also worth noting that layers are independent in that IP may be transported over Ethernet as in the model below, but can also be transported over any Layer 1 and Layer 2 medium, such as PPP (also Layer 2) over X.21 (Layer 1).

Given the model in figure 4-1, Ethernet is often referred to as a Layer 2 service and IP is often referred to as a Layer 3 service.

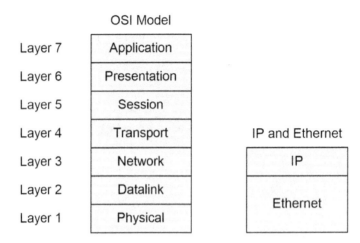

Figure 4-1, IP and Ethernet in Relation to the Seven Layer OSI Model

Ethernet Frame Classification

Throughout this book we have used the term packet to describe small blocks of data. In Layer 2 Ethernet terminology, a packet is more accurately referred to as a frame. For the purpose of this book, however, the terms packet and frame can be used interchangeably and essentially mean the same thing.

Ethernet has become the dominant Layer 1 and Layer 2 medium. It is a very versatile technology that can be delivered over fiber at great distance, copper cabling called category 5 and category 6 cabling, as well as standard telephony copper cables. Ethernet is present in virtually every enterprise LAN. It is very cheap and scales to 100Gbps, with work on-going to increase this further. Driven by demand from the enterprise sector for lower cost and higher bandwidth, Ethernet is becoming increasingly more widespread in the Service Provider WAN space.

Ethernet technology has been around for a long time. Initial work started by Xerox PARC was ready for standards review by March 1974. Early Ethernet deployments had no provision for traffic classification, and we must look to further Ethernet developments in which a traffic class field was added to the structure of Ethernet. One such development is described in an Institution of Electrical and Electronic Engineers

(IEEE) specification, specifically IEEE 802.1Q. First published in 1998, IEEE 802.1Q sets out a scheme to divide a single physical LAN into multiple separate LANs. This is done through a logical partition of the physical LAN and so they are referred to as Virtual LANs or VLANs.

The structure of an Ethernet Frame and the IEEE 802.1Q extensions are shown in figure 4-2.

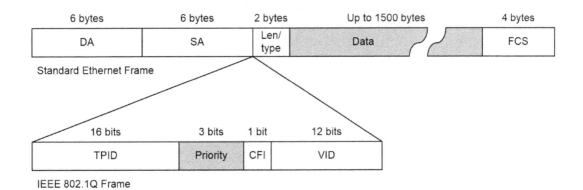

Standard Ethernet Frame

DA: Destination MAC address
SA: Source MAC address
Len/type: Frame length or Ethertype
Data: The user data
FCS: Frame Check Sequence

IEEE 801.2Q Extensions

TPID: Tag Protocol Identifier (usually x8100)
Priority: IEEE 802.1p class of service
CFI: Canonical Format Indicator (always zero for Ethernet)
VID: VLAN ID

Figure 4-2, The Ethernet and IEEE 802.1Q Frame Structures

Our focus will be on the Priority field. IEEE 802.1Q sets aside three bits specifically to identify a CoS for a Layer 2 'IEEE 802.1Q tagged' Ethernet frame. The IEEE 802.1Q frame or tag is inserted between the source MAC address field and the Length/Type field of a standard 'untagged' Ethernet frame. IEEE 802.1Q does not define how the priority field is used, so this is open to any implementation or interpretation. However, the IEEE did put forward a scheme for how the priority field can be used. They defined this scheme in IEEE 802.1p. This scheme is now generally accepted across the industry, but it is still only a recommendation. Any network administrator can choose to ignore it or define their own Layer 2 CoS scheme. It is worth noting that the work of the IEEE 802.1p task group finished in 1998 and IEEE 802.1p was incorporated into IEEE 802.1Q standard.

Three binary bits in the priority will give us eight permutations or eight CoS definitions. IEEE 802.1p interprets these definitions as given in the table 4-1.

CoS level	Binary	Purpose
7	111	Network
6	110	Internet
5	101	Critical
4	100	Flash-override
3	011	Flash
2	010	Immediate
1	001	Priority
0	000	Routine

Table 4-1, The Initial Recommended IEEE 8021p Scheme

The descriptions against the CoS levels are somewhat vague and were redefined in 1998, with the new definitions reflecting modern service classifications. These are set out in the table 4-2. 'Excellent Effort' being, in fact, 'CEO's best Effort' or 'best effort for your most valued customers'.

User_priority	Acronym	Traffic Type
1	BK	Background
2	--	Spare
0	BE	Best Effort
3	EE	Excellent Effort
4	CL	Controlled Load
5	VI	'Video' < 100 ms latency and jitter
6	VO	'Voice' < 10 ms latency and jitter
7	NC	Network Control

Table 4-2, The 1998 IEEE 802.1p Classification Scheme

IPv4 Packet Classification

Ethernet resides at layers 1 and 2 of the OSI model. The Internet and Service Provider's IP networks are Layer 3 networks. There are separate means to classify traffic within the Layer 3 Internet Protocol (IP).

IPv4 is almost ubiquitous in the LAN and the WAN. It is the Layer 3 protocol of choice for nearly all Enterprise organizations and certainly all Service Providers. The most widely deployed version of IP is version 4 (IPv4). IPv4 is defined in RFC 791 and was standardized in 1981. Figure 4-3 shows the relatively complicated IPv4 packet structure.

+	Bits 0 - 3	Bits 4 - 7	Bits 8 - 15	Bits 16 -18	Bits 19 - 31
0	Version	Header Length	Type of Service	Total Length	
32	Identification			Flags	Fragment Offset
64	Time to Live		Protocol	Header Checksum	
96	Source Address				
128	Destination Address				
160	Options				
160 or 192	Data				

Figure 4-3, The IPv4 Packet Structure

The field we need to focus on is the third in the IP header. This is called the Type of Service Field and is set aside for packet classification. RFC 791 made a recommendation as to how this field should be populated. Like the Priority field in the IEEE 802.1Q header, this is only a recommendation and any user can implement their own classification scheme if needed. The scheme defined in RFC 791 is referred to as IP Precedence. IP Precedence has largely been superseded by a new scheme defined in the Differentiated Services Model called the Differentiated Services Code Point (DSCP). DSCP is partially backward compatible with IP Precedence.

IP Precedence

The Type of Service (ToS) field, as defined in RFC 791, is shown in figure 4-4.

0	1	2	3	4	5	6	7
IP Precedence			D	T	R	0	0

Bits 0-2:   Precedence
Bit 3:   0 = Normal Delay, 1 = Low Delay
Bits 4:   0 = Normal Throughput, 1 = High Throughput
Bits 5:   0 = Normal Reliability, 1 = High Reliability
Bit 6-7:   Reserved for Future Use

Figure 4-4, The 8 Bits of the ToS Field in RFC 791 or IP Precedence

Figure 4-4 shows the eight bits of the ToS field. This scheme is referred to as IP Precedence. Bits 3, 4 and 5 (Delay, Throughput and Reliability) are hardly ever used and have no relevance for QoS in modern networks. The key elements are bit 0 through to bit 2. These three bits will give us eight CoS levels. RFC 791 defines some values for this field and these are shown in the table 4-3.

IP Precedence	Binary	Purpose
7	111	Network Control
6	110	Inter-network Control
5	101	CRITIC/ECP
4	100	Flash-override
3	011	Flash
2	010	Immediate
1	001	Priority
0	000	Routine

Table 4-3, Class of Service Levels as Defined in RFC 791

These definitions are very similar to those defined in IEEE 802.1p. This is no coincidence as there will certainly be a need to map Layer 2 CoS into Layer 3 CoS and vice versa. Consistency will only facilitate end to end QoS.

The Differentiated Services Field

The Differentiated Services (DS) field is part of the Differentiated Service (DiffServ) Architecture. The DS field is given specific treatment in RFC 2474. The DiffServ Architecture is set out in RFC 2475 and reviewed in chapter 7. Both RFCs are related and were standardized in December 1998.

RFC 2475 re-defines the ToS Field set out in RFC 791. The demand in the data communications industry was for more granular CoS definitions. This meant that more than eight levels or 3 bits would be required. Furthermore, it was recognized that bits 3 through to 5 (Delay, Throughput and Reliability) were never going to be used. Figure 4-5 shows the DS as defined in RFC 2474.

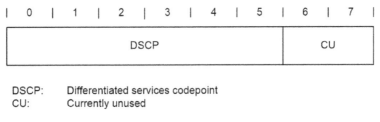

DSCP: Differentiated services codepoint
CU: Currently unused

Figure 4-5, The Differentiated Service Field

The DS field allocates the first 6 bits of the ToS field for traffic classification. These bits are referred to as the Differentiated Services Code Point (DSCP). There are 64 possible traffic classes using 6 bits. Neither RFC 2474 nor RFC 2475 define the values or behaviors associated with DSCP. This is work was undertaken in later RFCs, which are covered later in chapter 7 (The Differentiated Services Architectural model).

The last two bits of the DS field, defined in RFC 2474, are currently unused. However, they have since been allocated for the flow control of IP traffic.

IPv6 Traffic Classification

There is much talk about IP version 6 (IPv6), but the current deployment in the Internet is small compared to IPv4. However, with IPv4 address space now essentially exhausted, IPv6 will soon become dominant. Figure 4-6 shows the IPv6 header.

+	Bits 0 - 3	Bits 4 - 11	Bits 12 - 31		
0	Version	Service Class	Flow Label		
32	Payload Length			Next Header	Hop Limit
64	Source Address				
96					
128					
160					
192	Destination Address				
224					
256					
288					

Figure 4-6, The IPv6 Header

The IPv6 header is simpler than the IPv4 header. Eight bits in the Service Class are set aside for traffic classification. IPv6 is defined in RFC 2460. RFC 2460 does not specify a scheme, but clearly the existing IPv4 Precedence and DS field can be applied to these eight bits to provide a consistent Layer 3 CoS methodology.

Multi-Protocol Label Switching (MPLS)

No book looking at the latest QoS technologies would be complete without at least mentioning Multi-Protocol Label Switching (MPLS), if only to dispel some of the misconceptions about MPLS 'giving you QoS'.

Without going into the technology, it is true to say that MPLS is one technology that can be used to deliver QoS. MPLS was developed to facilitate 'traffic engineering' over Packet switching networks. It turns a connectionless network (i.e. packet switching) into a connection-oriented network. These MPLS based connections are called Label Switch Paths (LSPs). RSVP is used with MPLS and some extensions to standard

Interior Routing Protocols such as OSPF and IS-IS, to allow a user to control the path data will take through a network. QoS is achieved on the basis that RSVP instructs MPLS enabled routers to set aside resources such as bandwidth for a specific LSP.

The issue we have today is that MPLS based traffic engineering is not widely deployed. MPLS has found favor as a basis to deliver Virtual Private networks (VPNs) at both Layer 2 and Layer 3. This is because LSPs are private, and like ATM and Frame Relay, provide a means to logically partition a single physical network into multiple Virtually Private Networks. The issue here is that VPN technologies do not use any of the traffic engineering technologies apart from MPLS. RSVP and the extensions to the IGPs are not used. LSPs are set up with no consideration to resource requirement or QoS.

Therefore, there needs to be some other means to classify traffic in an MPLS VPN environment. Like IP and Ethernet, we need to look to the header for the solution. The diagram below shows an MPLS header - often referred to as an MPLS shim. It is very small, with just 24 bits, and so does not add too much overhead to the traffic. Figure 4-7 shows the MPLS header.

Label: 20 bits
Experimental Field (EXP): 3 bits
Bottom of Stack: 1 bit
Time to Live (TTL): 8 bits

Figure 4-7, The MPLS Shim

The fact is that no specific field was introduced into MPLS for the purpose of traffic classification and subsequently QoS. The MPLS shim has a three-bit field called the Experimental field or EXP bits. One use of this field is to provide a means for traffic classification. Given the fact those three bits provide eight possible traffic classes, it is directly compatible with IP Precedence and Ethernet IEEE 802.1p. It is also compatible with the DSCP, in particular the Class Selector values (see chapter 7 for more on Class Selectors). In real network environments, we will see a manual mapping between the payload class (IEEE 802.1p, IP Precedence or DSCP) to the EXP bits. We are then still reliant on the same queuing and scheduling mechanisms deployed on the network to deliver QoS to native IP or Ethernet traffic. Therefore, QoS for an MPLS network is no better or worse than pure Ethernet or IP traffic.

Chapter 5: Packet Queuing and Scheduling

Packet classification is only part of the solution when it comes to delivering QoS. Packet Classification only 'marks' or classifies traffic for preferential treatment. Mechanisms are needed within network devices to deliver that preference – Queuing and Scheduling, and the technologies used to achieve this.

Many queuing schemes have been developed over the years, but in general those described below are relevant in modern networking equipment. This applies to Layer 3 routers, Layer 2 switches and Layer 2 Carrier Ethernet demarcation devices.

A queue is simply an area of memory on a network device that stores or buffers packets, should they arrive into a device faster than they can be transmitted out of that device. There will be multiple queues on a device, each serving different traffic classes, and the scheduler defines how those queues are serviced. This chapter goes on to look at some of the main scheduling schemes in some detail. There are numerous other schemes that have dropped out of favor for various reasons. However, the schemes that follow are likely to be encountered in today's packet switching networks.

First in First out Queuing

First in First out (FIFO) queuing is the simplest of all techniques. A FIFO queue usually comprises a single buffer, and the first packet arriving into the buffer is the first packet out. There is no prioritization of traffic within a FIFO queue. It is analogous to people queuing in a line. Figure 5-1 illustrates the FIFO concept.

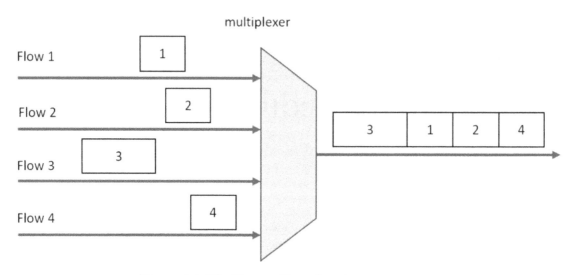

Figure 5-1, The First in First Out Queueing Concept

Priority Queuing

To understand priority queuing, it is worth taking time to look at an example where three priority queues are configured on the output of a network device. There may be more queues on real devices. The ability to have eight queues is common. However, the three queues in this example are called high priority, medium priority and low priority. Figure 5-2 illustrates three stages of traffic flow.

The system moves the packets to the appropriate queue based on their assigned class.

In this example, the high priority traffic is classified with the hatching pattern, the medium plain white, and the low priority traffic dotted. The flow into the system comprises a random sequence of packets that are presented to the system in no particular order of class. The system redirects traffic from each class to the appropriate queue and the scheduler then transmits traffic in strict order of priority. The highest priority traffic is always transmitted ahead of any lower priority traffic until that queue is exhausted. The next highest priority traffic is then transmitted and so on and so forth until all traffic is transmitted. However, if higher priority traffic enters a queue as a lower priority queue is being serviced, the scheduler stops work on the lower priority queue and transmits the higher priority traffic.

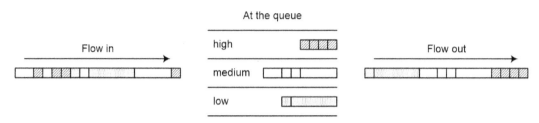

Figure 5-2, Priority Queuing

Priority queuing is great for voice traffic as we wish voice to have minimal delay and jitter. Voice traffic would be set for the highest data priority and so has minimum delay through the network device. Large data packets of lower priority are held back and so voice jitter is minimized.

The drawback of priority queuing is that it is strict in operation and so lower priority queues may never be serviced if higher priority traffic is present. This can lead to unacceptable performance for users of data applications that have low priority.

Weighted Round Robin

Along with Strict Priority Queuing, Weighted Round Robin (WRR) is often available on Layer 2 Ethernet switches and Layer 3 routers. It attempts to overcome the potential problem of the lower class traffic being starved of bandwidth by higher class traffic.

In order to understand WRR it is easier to first examine Round Robin Scheduling without the weighted element. Figure 5-3 shows the structure of a Round Robin queuing architecture.

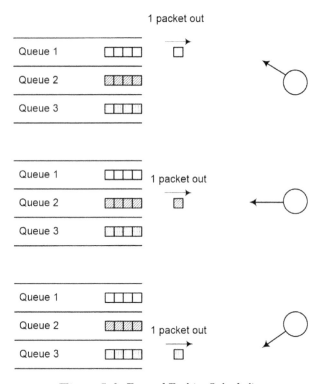

Figure 5-3, Round Robin Scheduling

Basic operation is simple. Packets or Ethernet Frames are placed in queues based on class. One packet is then de-queued in turn from each queue. When the last queue is serviced, then the cycle is repeated. A potential problem here is that one packet or frame at a time is de-queued, but packets and frames are variable in length. Therefore, it is possible that one queue may still acquire more bandwidth, although there is still an element of fairness. The main issue here is that traffic is not prioritized between classes. A weighted element can, however, be applied to the Round Robin scheduler to reflect priority or bandwidth needs. Figure 5-4 illustrates the Weighted Round Robin principle.

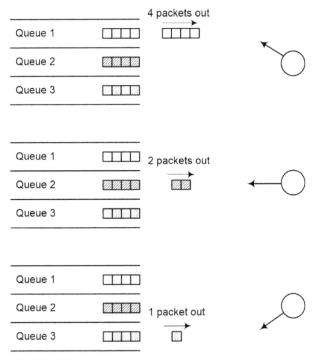

Figure 5-4, Weighted Round Robin Scheduling

A user can assign a weight to a queue in WRR scheduling. The weights in the above example are:

- Queue 1: 4
- Queue 2: 2
- Queue 3: 1

This means 4 packets are de-queued from queue 1, then 2 from queue 2 and then 1 from queue 3. The cycle is then repeated.

WRR gives the network administrator a high degree of control over how traffic classes are treated by the scheduler, with the bandwidth being effectively partitioned as needed. This works well when only data is being passed over the network, as business-critical applications can be given the greatest weight. However, IP voice is usually the highest priority and may use the lowest bandwidth. Therefore, applying weight to voice in this way may be problematic. Also, larger packets associated with the data in other queues means that any voice traffic may be subject to unacceptable jitter.

An effective compromise in modern Layer 2 switches and Layer 3 routers, is to combine Priority Queuing with WRR queuing. This methodology involves turning one WRR queue into a Priority Queue. Voice traffic is passed to this queue and is transmitted ahead of any traffic in the WRR queue. When this queue is empty, traffic in the WRR queues is transmitted. The WRR scheduler is interrupted if any traffic arrives in the Priority Queue.

Strict Priority with WRR is operationally very similar to Priority Queuing with Class Based Weighted Fair Queuing (discussed later). The two are often used to provide an end to end queuing mechanism over both Layer 2 and Layer 3 networks. This provides the high degree of consistent performance, and a common QoS policy can be applied to the whole network.

Weighted Fair Queuing (WFQ)

Fair Queuing is a technique derived from algorithms developed to facilitate the fair sharing of CPU processing time in general computing. The same principle can be applied to the transmission of data over a network. Fair Queuing is the easiest to configure, simply because it works automatically, underpinned by mathematical algorithms. However, that very fact also makes it more difficult to understand in detail. The weighted element in Weighted Fair Queuing is an extension to ordinary Fair Queuing which is IP Precedence or DSCP aware. This implies that WFQ only works at the IP packet level or Layer 3 of the OSI model.

The aim of WFQ is to provide both light and heavy network users with consistent response times. It is a flow-based queuing algorithm, and queuing decisions must be made on a flow by flow basis. In principle, low volume traffic flows receive preferential treatment and transmit their entire offered loads in a timely fashion, while high-volume traffic flows share the remaining capacity proportionally between them. The contents of the IP Header, including the ToS or DSCP field, are also used to derive traffic preference. The algorithm will examine each flow and make an estimate of the buffer it needs to allocate to each flow. This technique is called Packet-by-Packet Generalized Processor Sharing (PGPS). Ideally, you need one buffer or queue per flow and the network may need to provide for many thousands of WFQ queues per node. Once the queues are dynamically defined, the flows are placed in the respective queue. The algorithm then works out a slice of time set aside for scheduling that flow, thereby maintaining fairness. WFQ always drops packets from the most aggressive flows.

WFQ has the advantage of fairness and works quite well on low bandwidth links up to 2Mbps. However, it does have some drawbacks, which are listed below:

- It is not always possible to have one queue per flow
- It does not allow manual traffic classification
- It cannot provide fixed guarantees
- It has complex classification and scheduling mechanisms

Class Based – Weighted Fair Queuing (CB-WFQ)

Class Based Weighted Fair Queuing is an extension of the standard WFQ. The extensions provide support for user defined traffic classes. This is a very powerful Layer 3 router-based mechanism, as the traffic classes are defined by a comprehensive range of features including port, source IP, destination IP, DSCP, IP Precedence or even specific applications. The key to understanding the benefits of CB-WFQ is that traffic classification also extends to the allocation of a specific bandwidth to the class. A single queue is then assigned to each defined traffic class. The bandwidth allocated to the class is the minimum it will receive during congestion.

CB-WFQ addresses many of the shortcomings of WFQ. By handing control back to the network administrator, manual traffic classification is allowed. It is not flow based, so has simpler scheduling mechanisms and finally, fixed guarantees can be given to each class. The concept is that traffic of the same class gets the same treatment and so a single queue will be required per class.

The fixed guarantees are delivered in the form of the percentage of the bandwidth set aside for each class. These are minimum percentage bandwidths. Should a class not be transmitting or transmitting at a very low rate, another class can use that bandwidth, ensuring link efficiency.

The drawback is that the 'fairness' can still cause unacceptable delays to voice traffic. The ideal compromise is a scheme that combines Priority Queuing with Class Based – Weighted Fair Queuing. Figure 5-5 illustrates the concept of Class Based – Weighted Fair Queuing

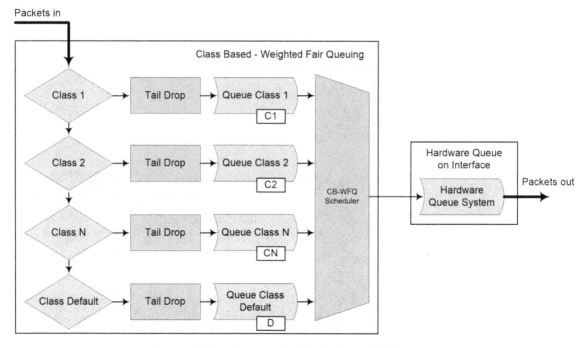

Figure 5-5, Class Based - Weighted Fair Queuing

Priority Queuing with Class Based – Weighted Fair Queuing (PQ-CBWFQ)

This form of queuing is also known as Low Latency Queuing (LLQ). LLQ is the preferred queuing mechanism used by most Service Providers in their core IP and MPLS networks.

LLQ takes Class Based – Weighted Fair Queuing and turns one queue only into a strict priority queue. This queue is set aside for low latency traffic, typically IP voice. The network administrator will still limit the traffic entering this queue to ensure that CB-WFQ queues are not starved of bandwidth. This is achieved by means of a 'traffic policer' located ahead of the priority queue.

Although voice will get appropriate treatment, it will still be discarded in favor of lower priority traffic if the traffic offered exceeds the rate configured on the policer. Service Providers will enter into a traffic contract to address the priority queue limits and apply extra cost to this traffic. This ensures that the end customer considers the bandwidth requirements and it passes responsibility for 'tuning' the bandwidth allocations to the end customer. This approach also means the end customer will not intentionally mark all their data traffic as 'voice traffic'. If they did, they will only end up harming all their network traffic.

Figure 5-6 illustrates the concept of PQ-CBWFQ.

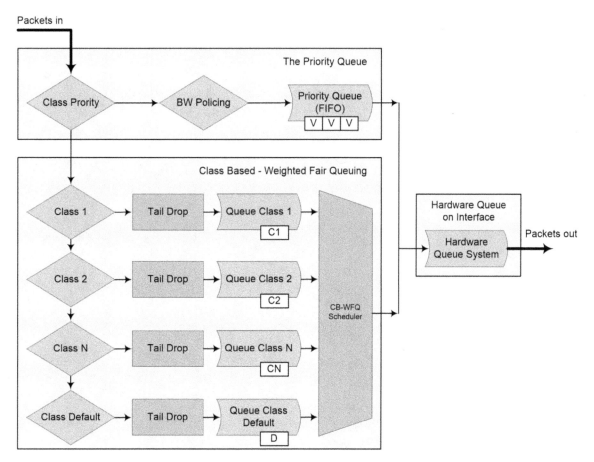

Figure 5-6, Priority Queuing with Class Based - Weighted Fair Queuing

Chapter 6: Congestion Avoidance

Congestion avoidance is a useful technique to provide QoS over packet switching, specifically IP, networks. It helps address the problem of Global Synchronization that is associated with TCP/IP traffic running over an oversubscribed network.

Any queue or buffer will become full if the user constantly tries to force more traffic into a network at a rate greater than it can be transported to its destination. The Transport Control Protocol (TCP) resides at Layer 4 of the OSI model. TCP is a session control protocol. Its purpose is to ensure data integrity. It detects transmission errors and lost packets, resolving these errors by requesting retransmissions and initiating flow control.

It is beyond the scope of this book to explain the operation of TCP in detail. However, in summary, if TCP detects packet loss, it will retransmit the data, but at a reduced rate. After a period of time, the rate is increased until the full transmission rate is once again achieved. In this way, TCP may alleviate network congestion. This mechanism is referred to as TCP 'slow start'. Problems can occur when networks are scaled from enterprise class networks to those needed as a Service Provider.

The network devices in a Service Provider network need to deal with hundreds and thousands of concurrent flows, each with its own TCP session. When heavy network congestion is encountered, irrespective of what queuing technique is used, the buffer will fill up. Once full, buffers must 'tail drop' data irrespective of class or priority. Each TCP session will initiate slow start procedures and slow down the re-transmission rate.

Each TCP session will realize that network congestion is no longer present at this slower rate, and all will start to increase their transmission rate at roughly the same time. When they hit full rate, the same network congestion is repeated, tail drops occur, and the TCP cycle is repeated. This process leads to the 'saw tooth' traffic pattern shown in figure 6-1. The phenomenon is referred to as 'Global Synchronization'. In figure 6-1, three sessions are started at different times and their slow start processes become synchronized over time.

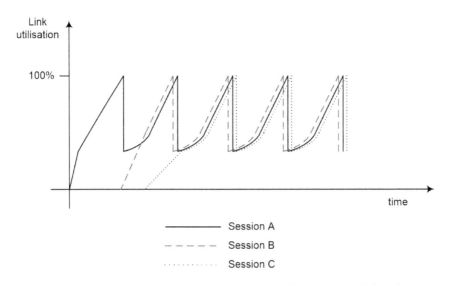

Figure 6-1, The Saw Tooth Traffic Profile Associated with Global Synchronization

Global Synchronization causes unacceptable network performance for data applications and is unique to TCP due to its flow control mechanism. TCP is not the only Layer 4 protocol used with IP. There would be no benefit to real time applications such as voice or video to retransmit lost data or have flow control. The User Datagram Protocol (UDP), on the other hand, does not support flow control nor error checking, and this makes it suitable for use as the Layer 4 protocol for IP voice and video instead of TCP.

Although not susceptible to global synchronization, there would benefit for real time traffic if network congestion is avoided. After all, QoS, especially on high speed networks, is only needed if the network is congested.

Random Early Detection (RED) and an augmented version called Weighted Random Early Detection (WRED) are congestion avoidance mechanisms designed to prevent queues from becoming full, so avoiding tail drops and subsequently, global synchronization.

Figure 6-2 will help to explain the operation of RED without the weighted element.

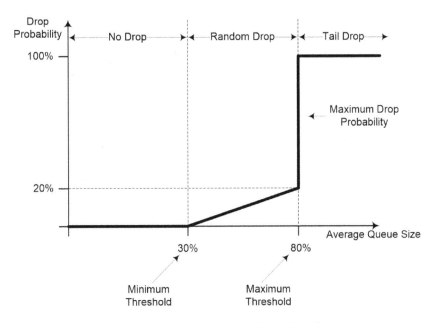

Figure 6-2, A Typical RED Profile

Referring to the graph above, RED monitors the size of a queue. At queue depths below 30%, RED will take no action but at a set minimum threshold (30% in figure 6-2), RED will start to drop packets randomly. Dropping a single or few packets randomly will only affect one or very few flows and the affected flows are the only ones which will initiate slow start procedures. This may well be enough to alleviate any congestion and so prevent global synchronization. If the queue continues to fill, then the drop probability increases. This means an increasing number of packets are dropped at random, affecting more flows, but still not all. If the queue still continues to fill, the user can configure a maximum queue threshold, beyond which all packets in that queue will be dropped. This is set to 80% in the above example. The above thresholds are only an example and can be configured by the user.

But why would you set a threshold of 80%, beyond which all packets are dropped, even though there is still spare capacity? The answer lies in Weighted RED (WRED). In practical systems, there will be more than one queue. Typically, there are four or more queues and selected traffic classes are forwarded to the respective queue. WRED allows a user to define a different drop profile for each queue and therefore, each traffic class. Lower minimum and maximum thresholds would be set for lower traffic classes. Therefore, the highest priority traffic will be the last to be affected. Figure 6-3 illustrates a set of WRED drop profiles.

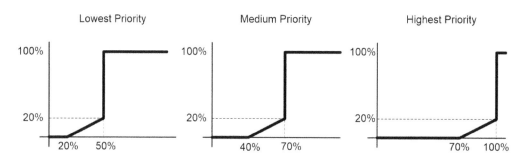

Figure 6-3, Example WRED Profiles

Chapter 7: The Differentiated Services Architectural Model

The basic problem of the IntServ model comes down to the scalability issues associated with RSVP in a Service Provider carrier class IP network. Reservations are made on a per flow basis. This fine degree of QoS is not necessarily needed - after all, why not just examine a packet's traffic class and then make a forwarding decision based on that class and not per flow. For example, all voice packets from all customers should be forwarded with low latency and low jitter, so there is no need to treat each voice flow individually.

The Differentiated Services (DiffServ) Architecture is defined in RFC 2475 (December 1998). Like the IntServ model, RFC 2475 provides a framework for delivering QoS over packet switching networks.

The approach taken by DiffServ makes sense. If you are able to mark or classify traffic at the edge and you have well known and understood queuing and scheduling techniques, then why do you need to signal QoS when each router or switch in the network can make forwarding decisions locally, based on the traffic class it receives. These local traffic forwarding behaviors are the key to DiffServ. They are called Per-Hop Behaviors (PHB) and their operation is simple: traffic is classified using the DSCP and then forwarded to an appropriate queue based on one of the techniques described previously.

As mentioned earlier, RFC 2474 redefined the IPv4 ToS field, replacing IP Precedence with 6 DiffServ Code Points (DSCP). The meaning of the DSCP was not defined in RFC 2474. It was essential that this work was done to help Service Providers offer consistent end to end QoS over their packet switching networks. RFC 3246 (March 2002) and RFC 2597 (June 1999) provided a definition for PHBs that are becoming the accepted standard for the industry. However, there is still no obligation for any Service Provider to adopt these PHBs.

The PHBs are called Expedited Forwarding, Assured Forwarding and Default. A fourth PHB called The Class Selector was introduced for backward compatibility with IP Precedence.

The Default class must always be present and is defined as part of RFC 2474. Any traffic that does not meet an Expedited Forwarding or Assured Forwarding class is forwarded within the Default PHB. All traffic within the Default class is usually 'best efforts' only with no guarantees.

Traffic within the Expedited Forwarding (EF) Class is forwarded with low loss, low latency and low jitter – so traffic that fits this profile would be voice and video. To achieve these characteristics, a Strict Priority queue is often used by the Layer 2 switch or Layer 3 router. The Service Provider would limit the quantity of EF traffic by means of a policer. Typically, the maximum would be 30% of the bandwidth so as not to allow EF traffic to starve Assured Forwarding (AF) traffic. Packets within the EF class are usually given the DSCP value of binary 101110 (decimal 46).

Assured Forwarding allows the operator to provide assurance of delivery if the traffic does not exceed some subscribed rate. Traffic that exceeds the subscription rate, however, faces a higher probability of being dropped if congestion occurs. RFC 2597 defines four separate AF classes and there are three levels of drop precedence within each class. This yields 12 different DSCP values for class and drop precedence as shown in the table 7-1.

Drop Precedence	Class 1	Class 2	Class 3	Class 4
Low	AF11	AF21	AF31	AF41
Medium	AF12	AF22	AF32	AF42
High	AF13	AF23	AF33	AF43

Table 7-1, DSCP Values for Class and Drop Precedence

A form of Class Based - Weighted Fair Queuing or Weighted Round Robin queuing would be applied the all AF classes to ensure no class can hog the queue.

Prior to DiffServ and the DSCP, routers could use the IP Precedence value to make forwarding decisions. In order to maintain backward compatibility with network devices that still use the Precedence field, DiffServ defines the Class Selector PHB. The Class Selector (CS) code-points are of the form 'xxx000', where the first three bits are the IP precedence bits and each IP precedence value can be mapped into a DiffServ class. If a packet is received from a non-DiffServ aware router that used IP precedence markings, the DiffServ router can still understand the encoding as a Class Selector code-point.

The associated DSCP values for AF class and Class Selector (CS) are shown in table 7-2.

CS1	001000
AF11	001010
AF12	001100
AF13	001110
CS2	010000
AF21	010010
AF22	010100
AF23	010110
CS3	011000
AF31	011010
AF32	011100
AF33	011110
CS4	100110
AF41	100010
AF42	100100
AF43	100110

Table 7-2, DSCP Values for AF Classes and Class Selector

Chapter 8: Layer 2 Ethernet Networks and the Metro Ethernet Forum

Much of the discussion so far has focused on the many techniques developed for Layer 3 routed environments. However, the business drivers are generating demand for higher bandwidth at lower cost. Ethernet is the ideal technology to deliver these business goals, but Ethernet is traditionally an enterprise technology. If Service Providers are to adopt it, particularly in the local access and metropolitan space, then there would need to be a significant number of extensions developed. The Metro Ethernet Forum (MEF) comprises over 200 organizations - equipment manufacturers, service providers and software providers. The original purpose of the MEF was to develop technical specifications and implementation agreements to promote interoperability and deployment of Carrier Ethernet worldwide. This purpose has now changed somewhat to reflect today's network transformation needs. Its stated objective is now to become the driving force enabling agile, assured and orchestrated communication services, that empower users with the dynamic performance and security required to thrive in the digital economy. For the purpose of this book, we will focus on the original aims of the MEF and look at some of the engineering specifications they developed to provide QoS within Carrier Ethernet environments.

One aspect of this work involves the introduction of QoS techniques for the Metro-Ethernet space. This is covered in the MEF specification MEF 10.3 (Ethernet Services Attributes Phase 3).

The approach taken by the MEF is to use traffic metering (often called 'traffic policing') as an admission control mechanism. This is just one component of QoS in Layer 2 Ethernet networks, the others being congestion avoidance, queuing and scheduling. The traffic metering concepts are very similar to those used by ATM and Frame Relay and the basic idea is that specific ports, VLANs or traffic types (that based on IEEE 802.1p, IP Precedence or DSCP) are given a specific guaranteed data rate. Traffic exceeding the guaranteed rate may be allowed onto the network if the capacity is available, but without any guarantee that it will be delivered. The MEF has defined some policer parameters that will help to explain the operation.

- **Committed Information Rate (CIR)**: The CIR is a Bandwidth Profile parameter. It defines the average rate in bits per second of service frames up to which the network delivers the service frames, and meets the performance objectives defined by the SLA
- **Excess Information Rate (EIR)**: The EIR is a Bandwidth Profile parameter. It defines the average rate in bits per second of service frames up to which the network may deliver the service frames, but without any performance objectives. i.e. it may or may not meet the SLA
- **Committed Burst Size (CBS)**: The CBS is a Bandwidth Profile parameter. It limits the maximum number of bytes available for a burst of service frames sent at the User to Network Interface (UNI) speed. Bytes under this limit remain CIR conformant
- **Excess Burst Size (EBS)**: The EBS is a Bandwidth Profile parameter. It limits the maximum number of bytes available for a burst of service frames sent at the UNI speed. Bytes under this limit remain EIR conformant

MEF 10.3 also introduces the concept of 'packet coloring'. The color of a packet is an indication of its level of conformance with a bandwidth profile or SLA.

- **Green Packets**: If the frames conform to the CIR of the bandwidth profile, they are marked green and delivered in accordance with the service performance objectives specified in the SLA
- **Yellow Packets**: If the frames are over the CIR and below the excess rate of the bandwidth profile, they are marked yellow

- **Red Packets**: If the frames do not conform to either the CIR or the EIR of the bandwidth profile, they are marked red and are usually discarded immediately

The parameters above are used within the metering technology. MEF 10.3 defines three forms of metering called:

- Two-rate, three color metering
- Single-rate, three color metering
- MEF-10.3 hierarchical policing with token-sharing envelopes

Two Rate, Three Color Metering

The CIR, EIR, CBS and EBS parameters are used within two-rate, three color metering (often called Twin Rate metering).

The CIR is the average rate up to which Ethernet frames are marked green. Green frames are called CIR conformant.

The EIR specifies the average rate up to which Ethernet frames are admitted to the Service Provider's network and the EIR is always greater than or equal to the CIR. Frames that exceed the CIR but are below the EIR are marked yellow. Because these frames do not conform to the CIR, the Service Provider does not provide any SLA guarantees regarding their delivery. Frames that exceed the EIR are regarded as non-conformant and are marked red. Red frames are typically discarded on ingress.

Since traffic levels can fluctuate, data traffic is 'bursty' in nature. The two-rate, three color metering process enables the traffic to burst above the CIR and EIR by a certain amount before marking the packets yellow and red respectively. This is easier on TCP traffic as it will be less prone to traffic drops, re-transmissions and TCP slow start. This burst capability is defined by the CBS and EBS parameters. It should be noted however, that the larger the CBS or EBS values, the more delay will be introduced to the traffic should these buffers fill.

With respect to two-rate metering, the CBS is defined as the maximum number of bytes allowed for incoming frames to burst above the CIR, but still be marked green. EBS is defined as the maximum number of bytes allowed for incoming frames to burst above the EIR and still be marked yellow. When the burst size has been exceeded, frames above the EIR are marked red.

A 'token bucket' analogy is often used to describe the twin-rate algorithm. The algorithm itself decides whether traffic conforms to a bandwidth profile defined by the CIR, EIR, CBS and EBS value. Traffic is then colored accordingly.

The token bucket analogy uses two buckets. One called the C-Bucket and the other called the E-Bucket. They have volumes equal to the CBS and EBS values respectively. This concept is shown in figure 8-1.

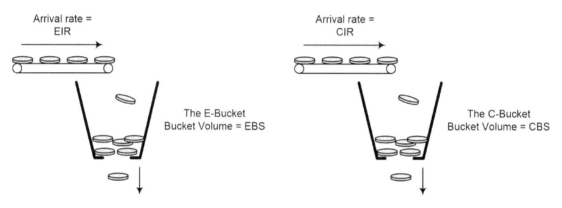

Figure 8-1, The Two-rate, Three Color Token Bucket Analogy

Tokens are dropped into the C-Bucket at a rate equal to the CIR and tokens are dropped into the E-Bucket at a rate equal to the EIR. Simultaneously, every time an Ethernet frame goes past, a set of tokens equal to the size of the frame are taken out of the buckets. If the C-Bucket is not empty, frames are marked with the color green. When the C-Bucket is empty, but the E-Bucket is not, then frames are marked with the color yellow. If both buckets are empty, then frames are marked red and usually discarded. The flow chart in figure 8-2 summarizes this process.

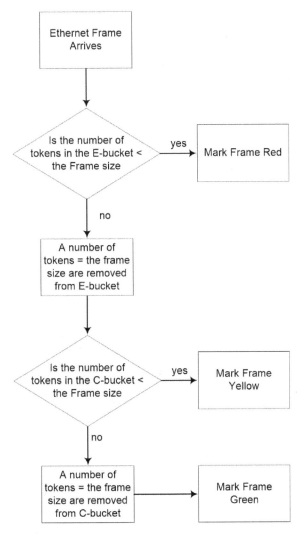

Figure 8-2, The Two Rate, Three Color Token Analogy Flow Chart

Single Rate, Three Color Metering

Another common algorithm is called Single Rate, Three Color Metering (often called Single Rate Metering). Within Single Rate metering, only a single bandwidth limit is set, but two burst sizes are set. The Single Rate algorithm can also be explained by using the token bucket analogy. This is shown in figure 8-3.

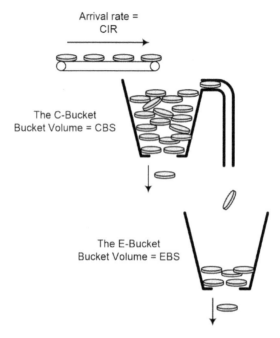

Figure 8-3, The Single Rate, Three Color Token Bucket Analogy

The Single Rate token bucket analogy still uses two buckets. The volume of the C-Bucket is equal to the CBS and the volume of the E-Bucket is equal to the EBS.

The C-Bucket is filled at a rate equal to the CIR. When the C-bucket is full, tokens flow into the E-bucket. Tokens are removed from the buckets when Ethernet frames pass through the system. Frames are marked green if the first bucket is not empty. Frames are marked yellow if the first bucket is empty, but the second is not. Finally, frames are marked red when both buckets are empty. A flow chart in figure 8-4 summarizing this information.

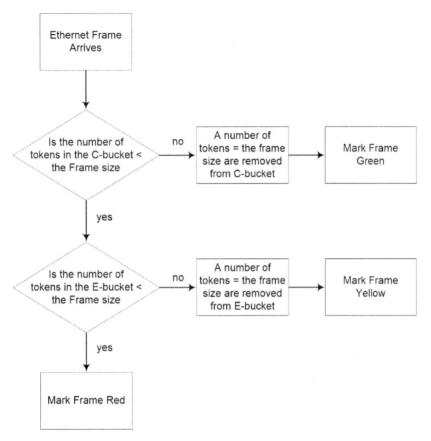

Figure 8-4, The Single Rate, Three Color Token Analogy Flow Chart

MEF 10.3 Policing

MEF 10.3, Ethernet Service Attributes phase 3 introduced a new policer concept. In addition to the CIR, EIR, EBS and CBS, there are four new attributes to consider. These are the CIR_{max}, EIR_{max}, Envelope and Rank. These new attributes are defined as follows:

- CIR_{max} is the Bandwidth Profile parameter that limits the rate of tokens added to the committed token bucket
- EIR_{max} is the Bandwidth Profile parameter that limits the rate of tokens added to the excess token bucket

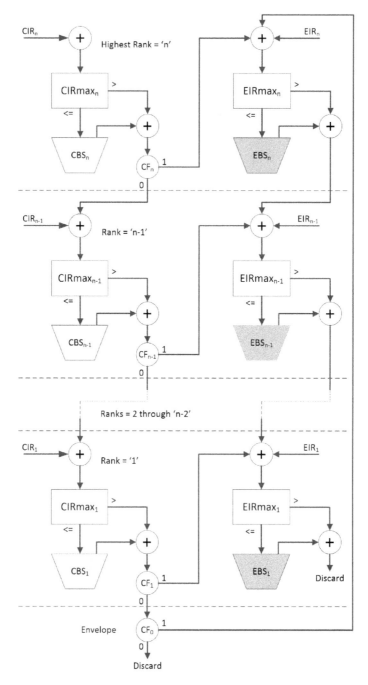

Figure 8-5, MEF 10.3 Policing

The Envelope is a set of 'n' Bandwidth Profile Flows in which each Bandwidth Profile Flow is assigned a unique rank between 1 (lowest) and 'n' (highest).

The diagram in figure 8-5 shows an MEF 10.3 policer example comprising an envelope with 'n' ranks. Each Bandwidth Profile Flow is associated with a rank. A Bandwidth Profile Flow comprises a CBS and EBS bucket pair. Each Bandwidth Profile Flow behaves in the same way as the Single Rate, Three Color Metering.

The Coupling Flag has a new function within 10.3 policing. If set to 1, the Coupling Flag retains the existing Single Rate, Three Color Metering behavior of overflow of tokens from the CBS to EBS bucket. If set to 0, the Coupling Flag exhibits the new behavior. With this new behavior, overflow of tokens from the CBS bucket is to the CBS bucket of the next lowest rank.

- The CIR_{max} limits the total token rate added to a CIR bucket (Bandwidth Profile CIR plus Overflow CIR)
- The EIR_{max} limits the total token rate added to an EIR bucket (Bandwidth Profile EIR plus Overflow EIR)
- The Envelope has a Coupling-Flag from lowest rank CBS to highest rank EBS when set to 1

MEF 10.3 policing provides a mechanism to allow other Bandwidth Flow Profiles in the Envelope access to unused bandwidth whether that be CIR or EIR bandwidth. The rank of a Bandwidth Flow Profile will typically be associated with a CoS and reallocation of bandwidth is generally from higher to lower ranks or classes.

Color Aware and Color-Blind Modes

The above metering algorithms are all referred to as 'color blind'. That is, Ethernet frames are considered to have had no conformance judgement made on them before they arrive at the meter. Effectively, all packets are green when they enter the metering process and are only marked yellow or red if the traffic class exceeds the bandwidth limits on that device.

It is also possible to have a metering process work in color aware mode where the Ethernet frames have already been allocated a color by an upstream device before entering the metering process. For example, when a red frame enters the meter, it remains red. If a yellow frame enters the meter, it can be marked red if the max bandwidth and max burst size have been exceeded, otherwise it remains yellow. In color-aware mode the device should not remark non-conformant packets as conformant or green.

Chapter 9: Quality of Service in SD-WAN environments

There are several new technologies that are transforming how networks are delivered in the wide area and service provider domains. We are seeing traditional hardware-based equipment such as routers and firewalls being virtualized and run as software applications on generic x86 based servers. This transformation technology is referred to as Network Functions Virtualization. Also, Software Defined Networking (SDN) decouples traditional control plane functions such as routing protocols from network elements and replaces them with a centralized controller. SDN in the Wide Area Network (WAN) is another such transformation technology that replaces traditional routed networks but give rise to its own Quality of Service (QoS) challenges.

SD-WAN allows any first mile transport technology to be used to provide connectivity to the customer premises and 'any transport technology' can be traditional MPLS based access, LTE, public internet or any wholesale copper access. An SD-WAN solution will look to combine these access circuits to provide aggregated bandwidth or use them as back up option. The diagram in figure 9-1 illustrates the principle.

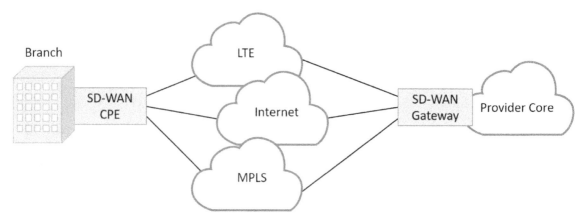

Figure 9-1, The SD-WAN Concept

In figure 9-1, the first mile transport comprises LTE, xDSL based Internet and a fixed MPLS based service. The SD-WAN solution will treat the various transport mechanisms as a pool of resources. These will be allocated to the service based on policies defined by the IT department of the end customer. Clearly, this is needed as the Internet, by its very nature, will not provide as good a QoS as the fixed MPLS access and so the policy may dictate that 'best efforts', low priority traffic uses this access. Mission critical traffic, meanwhile, can be allocated to the MPLS services. Most SD-WAN solutions allow this form of bandwidth allocation where the percentage of any access type can be assigned to a traffic class or even application based on TCP port. This policy assignment also allows traffic to be steered towards a form of access such as LTE. This essentially means that the traditional edge routing is no longer needed and traditional routing gives way to policy-based forwarding.

Policy based forwarding will help with QoS, but the per-hop treatment of QoS used by switches and routers no longer applies in the Internet, meaning that QoS markings are simply not honored. So, what can be done about this? Forward Error Correction (FEC) is a technology that allows a packet to be corrected for any errors rather the discarded. FEC does add overhead, but this can still lead to an overall improvement in throughput. With all TCP transmissions, there is a window size set by the protocol. The window is the number of packets that are transmitted before the receiver sends an acknowledgment. If packets are lost or corrupted, all the packets in the window will need to be retransmitted, leading to a reduction in throughput. Also, we need to consider the fact that TCP will reduce its transmission rate if packets are lost. FEC will certainly help reduce TCP packet loss and improve overall throughput.

Forward Error Correction

Forward Error Correction or FEC is the methodology for adding error control data to a packet stream. The transmitting end sends redundant data and the receiving end recognizes only the portion of the data that contains no apparent errors. Because FEC does not require handshaking between the source and the destination, it can be used for broadcasting of data to many destinations simultaneously from a single source.

In its simplest form, FEC sends each character twice. The receiver checks both instances of each character for adherence to the protocol being used. If conformity occurs in both instances, the character is accepted. If conformity occurs in one instance and not in the other, the character that conforms to protocol is accepted. If conformity does not occur in either instance, the character is rejected and a blank space or an underscore (_) is displayed in its place. This is referred or as Simple FEC. Simple FEC algorithms are inefficient, often requiring a 1:1 relationship between the data and the FEC code.

Hamming codes are another form of FEC algorithm and are named after Richard Hamming, who worked at Bell Labs in the late 1940s on the Bell Model V computer. Hamming codes can detect up to two-bit errors or can correct one-bit errors in a data stream by adding redundant bits to the data.

There are much more complex FEC algorithms in use today. The Reed-Solomon algorithm adds approximately 7% overhead to the data stream. Irving S. Reed and Gustave Solomon invented a series of Reed-Solomon FEC codes in 1960, and these are still used today in many technologies such as CDs, DVDs, Blu-ray Discs, QR Codes, data transmission technologies (such as DSL and Wireless), broadcast systems (such as satellite communications, DVB and ATSC) as well as storage systems (such as RAID 6).

There is no standard FEC algorithm applied to SD-WAN environment, and equipment vendors are therefore open to apply any existing algorithm or develop their own. As a direct result, this often means that vendor interworking is not possible – so FEC is often promoted as a unique selling point of their solution.

Chapter 10: Traffic Engineering

At the start of this book, we discussed the relative benefits of Circuit Switched and Packet Switched networks and determined that Circuit Switched networks had inherent QoS capabilities. These being, that when we establish a path or circuit over a network, we have control over the traffic flow. It has consistent latency and enough bandwidth to meet the needs of the traffic flow. Packet Switched network are just the opposite. Traffic in the flow may take a different route over paths of unequal bandwidth and this leads to the possibility of traffic loss and variable latency. Traffic engineering technologies effectively change the behavior of a Packet Switched network to that of a Circuit Switched network, simply by providing the means to ensure traffic takes the same route over the network and that enough bandwidth is set aside to meet the needs of that flow. In this chapter, we look at some of the legacy technologies and current technologies used to achieve what is called traffic engineering.

MPLS RSVP-TE

In chapter 3, we learnt about the Resource Reservation Protocol (RSVP). RSVP in the traffic engineering context, operates in the same way as in the Integrated Services QoS model. It does, however, have some extensions for traffic engineering. In MPLS RSVP-TE, RSVP works with MPLS to set up Label Switch Paths for traffic engineering. These paths are set up in a way that would manipulate the path such that the route would be different compared to one set up by native routing or Label Distribution Protocol

(LDP). The following describes the operation of RSVP-TE. The diagram in figure 10-1 shows four routers over which an RSVP-TE signaled LSP will be established.

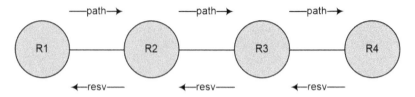

Figure 10-1, A Four Node RSVP-TE Example

R1 is the headend router. RSVP-TE is a source routing methodology and R1 will hold the network resource requirements for the path to R4. The LSP setup is initiated by headend router R1 and is identified as a session that specifies the destination router for the LSP (in this case R4), tunnel identifier, and an extended tunnel identifier.

The headend RSVP component signals a PATH message destined toward R4. The PATH message can include two key informational elements. These are the policy link-admission control information that identifies the sender that is setting up the path, and a flow specification that defines the resources that need allocating for the path.

Each hop along the path examines the PATH message and verifies the policy control information. Each hop then saves the path state that is associated with the session and sets aside the requested resources specified by the sender. When the destination router is reached, a hop-by-hop reservation (RESV) message is initiated by R4 and sent toward R1. The RESV message takes the same route back to the sender that the PATH message took from the headend to the destination.

At each node, including the destination, the session-state is updated, and the necessary resources are reserved for the session. An MPLS label is allocated for use by the prior hop. When the RESV message reaches the headend router, the LSP setup for the session is complete.

The reservation state must be periodically refreshed by sending new PATH messages to which there must be a RESV message in return. If these updates fail, RSVP signals an error, the path is torn down and the resources are released.

Constrained Shortest Path First (CSPF)

CSPF can be considered a legacy traffic engineering technology. However, it is worth mentioning. CSPF is an extension of the shortest path algorithm that is used in link state routing protocols such as OSPF and IS-IS. OSPF is a good example to take. With OSPF, each hop in a path is allocated a cost. For the example in figure 10-2, the shortest path to R6 from R1 is R1 to R2 to R5 and then to R6 since the total path cost is 30.

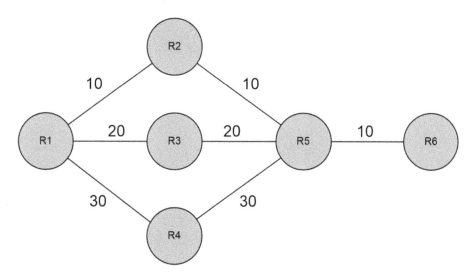

Figure 10-2, A Shortest Path First Example

The path cost for the route via R3 is 50 and the path cost for the route via R4 is 70. The path cost in real routing networks is automatically assigned based on the bandwidth of the links. However, this path cost can be edited and it is this flexibility in how a path cost can be allocated, that can be used to engineer the route traffic takes.

With CSFP we can assign a set of constraints to a link. Let's say we have a service with three quality levels: gold, silver and bronze. We assign these attributes to the same network as shown in figure 10-3.

What we can then do is assign a desired service level to a flow or a Label Switch Path if using MPLS. We can specify that a flow can only use links with gold attributes and this constraint overrides the SPF algorithm, meaning that traffic routes from R1 to R6 via R4.

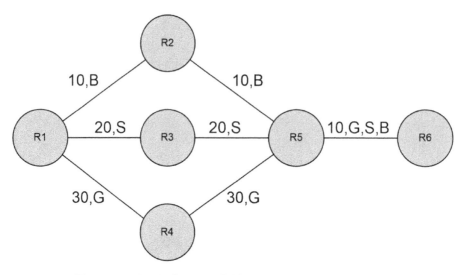

Figure 10-3, A Contained Shortest Path First Example

CSPF principles are as simple, in theory, as that!

RSVP-TE vs CSPF

If CSPF is so simple, then why is it not widely used in modern networks? The basic answer is that constraints need to be manually added to the network routers, which is not operationally sustainable as networks grow and it would be hard to track changes. With RSVP-TE there is a signaling mechanism and the resources requirement only needs to be added to the source of the flow, the rest being automated. RSVP itself does have to maintain path states, and it too has scalability constraints, but is deemed to be the preferred approach to traffic engineering within packet networks. However, there is a new technology that will provide the same traffic engineering benefits of RSVP-TE without the signaling overhead - and that technology is Segment Routing. Segment Routing is covered later in this chapter.

MPLS-TP

MPLS, or IP-MPLS as it is often referred to, is often used within traffic engineering to deliver QoS over packet networks. However, IP-MPLS does have its drawbacks that led some in the industry to question its carrier class credentials. IP-MPLS Label Switch Paths can be unpredictable and non-deterministic and this can be problematic when QoS is needed. The fundamental issue is that LSPs are unidirectional. The path from source to destination can be different to the path from destination to source, leading to variable latency and unpredictable performance.

Multi-Protocol Label Switching – Traffic Profile (MPLS-TP) was developed to address this, and other drawbacks associated with IP-MPLS. In MPLS-TP terms, LSPs that have the same path from source to destination, and destination to source, are referred to as congruent paths. The other drawbacks of IP-MPLS addressed with MPLS-TP are:

- Penultimate Hot Popping (PHP)
- Equal Cost Multipath (ECMP) routing
- LSP merge

We need to dig a little deeper to understand these issues. MPLS-TP does retain some of the key features of IP-MPLS - mainly, the ability to provide point-to-point pseudo-wire services and multi-point services such as those provided by Virtual Private LAN Services (VPLS). MPLS-TP also provides features for enhanced Operation Administration and Maintenance functions (OAM) and fast failover of less than 50ms.

IP-MPLS supports a feature called Penultimate Hop Popping (PHP), which provides a means to pop the MPLS label one hop before the destination. Envisage a case where all packets flow to a single gateway router. If we used ultimate hop popping, all LSPs will be terminated on that router. If there are a lot of LSPs, then that router will need to perform a lot of work popping the labels and that may impact performance. PHP means that the work can be shared by all the routers connected to that gateway. Therefore, the gains in performance may be worth the extra work needed to configure PHP on the network. The issue for MPLS-TP is that it provides end to end QoS, end to end OAM and fast failover. These benefits cannot be realized if the LSP is terminated on the penultimate hop, which means that the LSP will simply not be end to end.

Equal Cost Multipath (ECMP) routing allows multiple links to be used if more than one path from source to destination has the same path cost. Whilst this allows load sharing of traffic, it goes against a fundamental feature of MPLS-TP: to provide deterministic and congruent paths.

IP-MPLS provides the means to merge LSPs. If multiple LSPs traverse the same intermediate router and follow a common path at some point on the network, there is no need to maintain each LSP since those LSPs which share common paths can be merged, thus reducing the number of labels needed. From a MPLS-TP perspective, this would mean that each LSP would not be deterministic and it would be extremely hard work to understand the individual requirements of each LSP to deliver the OAM and failover features.

The fast reroute technology behind MPLS-TP is Bidirectional Forwarding Detection or BFD. BFD can be used to provide protection for other forwarding technologies such as EVCs, GRE tunnels and VXLAN tunnels. BFD has low overhead and it provides a consistent method of detecting failures over the multiple paths. This may not be the case if we use native routing protocols and as such, BFD provides deterministic failure detection. The figure 10-4 shows a basic BFD setup.

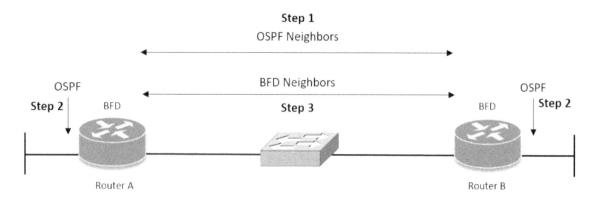

Figure 10-4, BFD Neighbors and Normal Operation

BFD establishes peer relationships between end points in a path. These end points will establish a neighbor relationship in normal operation. BFD is asynchronous, so BFD will need to be configured at each end point. When OSPF discovers a neighbor (step 1), it sends a request to the local BFD process to initiate a BFD neighbor session with the OSPF neighbor router (step 2). The BFD neighbor session with the OSPF neighbor router is established (step 3).

Figure 10-5 shows what happens if a failure is detected.

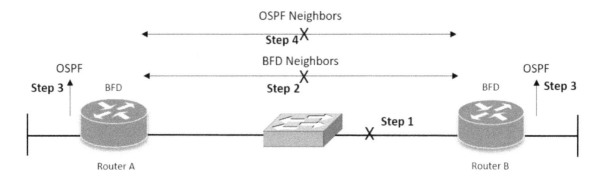

Figure 10-5, BFD in Failure Mode

In failure node, the BFD neighbor session with the OSPF neighbor router is torn down (step 2). BFD notifies the local OSPF process that the BFD neighbor is no longer reachable (step 3) and the local OSPF process then tears down the OSPF neighbor relationship (step 4). If an alternative path is available, the routers will immediately start converging on it.

Once a BFD session is established and timer negotiations are complete, BFD peers periodically send BFD control packets to detect liveliness. The rate of BFD packet exchange would be much greater than that associated with the IGP hello messages. It should be noted that BFD is a forwarding path failure detection protocol. BFD detects a failure, but the routing protocol must act to bypass a failed peer.

We need to consider MPLS-TP OAM. This provides a set of carrier class software tools to monitor and manage an MPLS-TP enabled network. MPLS-TP OAM messages are designed to travel on the exact same path that the data would take - in other words, MPLS-TP OAM monitors the Pseudo Wires or Label Switch Paths. Key to the transport of OAM messages in MPLS are the G-ACh and the Generic Alert Label (GAL). As their names indicate, they allow an operator to send any type of control traffic in a Pseudo Wire or LSP. The OAM capabilities of MPLS-TP are defined in ITU-T G.8113.1 (Operations, Administration and Maintenance Mechanisms for MPLS-TP in Packet Transport Networks). However, the OAM functionalities of MPLS-TP follow the same format and function as Y.1731 (discussed in chapter 11).

Segment Routing

Segment routing is a newer technological solution that can provide traffic engineering. It is described in RFC 8402, Segment Routing Architecture. The motivation for Segment routing was to provide a traffic forwarding technology suitable for operation within Software Defined Networks (SDN). It is argued that SDN is essential if networks are to meet the growth and performance demands needed for modern networks. Demand for bandwidth is growing and this increased bandwidth needs to be provided cheaply. Automation is one aspect of SDN that can reduce costs, as services can be defined centrally and be deployed using software tools that communicate with network elements using Application Programming Interfaces or APIs. This way of controlling networks is referred to as Network Orchestration. Having network engineers with XML and Java Script Object Notation (JSON) programming skills to work with some of the modern SDN APIs, is becoming more important than having traditional Command Line Interface skills.

The challenge that traditional IP-MPLS and IP routing technologies present in SDN environments, is that forward decisions are made by a control plane embedded within each network element. This is counter to the concepts of SDN, where network routes are defined by a central controller and this has opened the way for newer technologies better suited for SDN environments.

Segment Routing is one such technology. Segment Routing is a source routing technology, which means all the forwarding instructions are defined at the source node. As such, we can dispense with complex signaling protocols such as RSVP-TE and LDP that are prevalent in IP-MPLS networks.

Segment Routing also has some other attractions. In a Segment Routing network, a node steers a packet through an ordered list of instructions, called 'segments'. These segments are encoded as MPLS labels. The benefit is that existing MPLS control plane technology can be reused for Segment Routing. In theory, existing MPLS enabled routers should be able to support Segment Routing simply by applying a software upgrade.

Figure 10-6 is used to help explain the operation of Segment Routing.

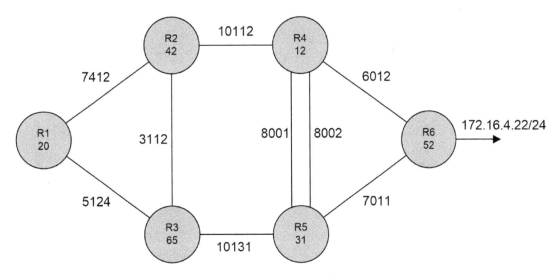

Figure 10-6, A Segment Routing Example

The portion of the network that runs Segment Routing can be split into Segment Routing domains. The premise behind the domain concept is to provide a means to limit the size of the label stack at the source router, which may be large if the domain is large. This may not be a problem by itself, but Maximum Transmission Unit or MTU size may become an issue.

For the example in figure 10-6, the Segment Routing domain comprises six routers, R1 to R6, with each router being assigned a Nodal ID. In our example we have the Nodal IDs as defined in table 10-1.

Router	Nodal ID
R1	20
R2	42
R3	65
R4	12
R5	31
R6	52

Table 10-1, Segment Routing Nodal ID Example

The links in the network are also assigned Adjacency IDs (shown in table 10-2.)

Link	Adjacency ID
R1 to R2	7412
R1 to R3	5124
R2 to R3	3112
R2 to R4	10012
R3 to R5	10131
R4 to R5	8001 and 8002
R4 to R6	6012
R5 to R6	7011

Table 10-2, Segment Routing Adjacency ID Example

Segment Routing works as follows. A packet needs to be routed from R1 to the server connected to R6 with the IP address 172.16.4.22/24. Once all the Nodal IDs and Adjacency IDs are assigned, they are distributed to all other routers using the IGP alone. There is no need for an MPLS signaling mechanisms such as LDP. The IGP also sends information about the bandwidth on any given link, as well as information on exception handling and load balancing requirements.

Segment Routing then uses a Path Computation Element (PCE, sometimes called Path Computation Engine) to calculate the path a packet needs to take to reach it destination. The PCE can reside on the source node or reside in an SDN controller and communicate with the node using APIs. The calculated path is represented by a series of MPLS like labels, which are pushed onto the packet in the form of a Segment Routing header. In our example, the Segment Routing header is shown in table 10-3, as we wish the packet to traverse the network via R2, R4, R5 (via link 8001) then R6.

42
12
8001
31
52

Table 10-3, The Segment Routing Header at R1

Each of the routers in the network will have a forwarding table. The forwarding table for R1 will look something like the one shown in table 10-4.

Destination Network	Segment ID	Interface
172.16.4.22.0/24	42	0.2

Table 10-4, The Forwarding Table at R1

R2 has a forwarding table which is much simpler than R1, and this is shown in table 10-5.

Incoming Segment ID	Outgoing segment ID	Interface
42	12	0.1

Table 10-5, The Forwarding Table at R2

Once the packet is forwarded to R2, the topmost label is popped. This leave the leaves stack at R2 as shown in table 10-6.

12
8001
31
52

Table 10-6, The Segment Routing Header at R2

The packet is forwarded to R4. The forwarding table of R4 is shown in table 10-7.

Incoming Segment ID	Outgoing segment ID	Interface
12	8001	0.3

Table 10-7, The Forwarding Table at R4

The packet has multiple options to reach R5, but the instructions given state it must take the link with adjacency ID 8001. Two labels are popped at R5: 12 and 8001. R5 knows it must pass the packet to nodal ID 52, i.e. R6. At R6 the final label is popped, and the packet sent to its destination.

In simple terms that is the basic operation of Segment Routing.

Chapter 11: Measuring Quality of Service in Network Environments

Implementing a Quality of Service strategy on a network is one thing, but how do you know that that QoS solution is working? If you are a Service Provider and contracted to an agreed service level, how do you measure the performance of the network and what tools do you have at hand to resolve customer related issues? In this chapter we look at some of the technologies available for measuring QoS in Layer 2 and Layer 3 packet networks.

Remote Network Monitoring (RMON)

RMON is a Management Information Base (MIB) developed by the Internet Engineering Task Force (IETF) that allows a network operator to monitor switches and routers in a network by applying software probes. It allows the operator to characterize the traffic and application flows at selected ports on a network element. The resultant data is typically accessed using the Simple Network Management Protocol (SNMP) and processed offline using performance reporting software tools. In simple terms, RMON statistics are counters for ports or virtual circuits. Basic elements consist of: frames passed, frame size and frame errors, amongst other things. Therefore, RMON statistics provide a snapshot of what is happening at that port or virtual circuit. RMON 2 is the latest version of RMON, and both RMON 1 and RMON 2 are defined by RFC 2819 and RFC 2021 respectively. These standards defined only 32-bit counters for the parameters, and this is a definite issue for modern high bandwidth Fast Ethernet (100Mbps) and Gigabit Ethernet ports. RFC 4502 therefore updated the standards to support 64-bit counters. Table 11-1 shows RMON 1 groups.

RMON 1 Group	Function	Elements
Statistics	Contains statistics measured by the RMON probe for each monitored interface on this device	Packets dropped, packets sent, bytes sent (octets), broadcast packets, multicast packets, CRC errors, runts, giants, fragments, jabbers, collisions, and counters for packets ranging from 64 to 128, 128 to 256, 256 to 512, 512 to 1024, and 1024 to 1518 bytes
History	Records periodic statistical samples from a network and stores them for later retrieval	Sample period, number of samples, items sampled
Alarms	Periodically takes statistical samples from variables in the probe and compares them with previously configured thresholds. If the monitored variable crosses a threshold, an event is generated	Includes the alarm table: alarm type, interval, starting threshold, stop threshold. Note: The Alarms group requires the implementation of the Events group
Hosts	Contains statistics associated with each host discovered on the LAN	Host MAC address, packets, and bytes received and transmitted, as well as number of broadcasts, multicast, and error packets
HostTopN	Prepares tables that describe the hosts that top a list ordered by one of their base statistics over an interval specified by the management station. Thus, these statistics are rate-based	Statistics, host(s), sample start and stop periods, rate base, and duration

RMON 1 Group	Function	Elements
Traffic Matrix	Stores statistics for conversations between sets of two MAC addresses. As the device detects a new conversation, it creates a new entry in its table	Source and destination MAC address pairs and packets, bytes, and errors for each conversation
Filters	Enables packets to be matched by a filter equation. These matched packets form a data stream that might be captured or that might generate events	Bit-filter type (mask or not mask), filter expression (bit level), conditional expression (and, or, not) to other filters
Packet Capture	Enables packets to be captured	Size of buffer for captured packets, full status (alarm), and number of captured packets
Events	Controls the generation and notification of events from this device	Event type, description, the last time the event was sent
Token Ring	Provides additional statistics for Token Ring networks	MAC Layer statistics, promiscuous statistics, MAC Layer history, promiscuous history, ring station order table, alarms, events

Table 11-1 RMON 1 Groups

Table 11-2 shows RMON 2 groups.

RMON 2 Group	Function
protocolDir	Lists the protocols supported by the RMON probe. Allows the addition, deletion, and configuration of entries in this list
protocolDist	Shows statistics (number of octets and packets) on a per-protocol basis
addressMap	Lists MAC address to network address bindings and the interface they were last seen on
nlHost	Network Layer Host group. Counts the amount of traffic sent from and to each discovered network address
nlMatrix	Network Layer Matrix group. Counts the amount of traffic sent between each pair of discovered network addresses
alHost	Application Layer Host group. Counts the amount of traffic, per protocol, sent from and to each discovered network address
alMatrix	Application Layer Matrix group. Counts the amount of traffic, per protocol, sent between each pair of discovered network addresses
usrHistory	User History group. Combines mechanisms from the Alarms and History groups to provide history collection based on user-defined criteria
probeConfig	Controls the configuration of RMON features
rmonConformance	Describes conformance requirements

Table 11-2 RMON 2 Groups

Cisco NetFlow and IPFIX (RFC 7011)

Developed by Cisco in the mid 1990s, NetFlow is an embedded application within Cisco IOS Software to characterize network operation. It can run at the port level on routers and switches, and provides deep packet inspection giving network administrators a comprehensive understanding of what is running over a network. This information can be used to fine-tune QoS policies. Processing of NetFlow can provide the following:

- Application and network usage
- Network productivity and utilization of network resources
- The impact of changes to the network
- Network anomaly and security vulnerabilities
- Long term compliance issues

NetFlow is a Cisco proprietary technology and runs on Cisco platforms. However, it became the de facto standard by which other vendors provided similar functionality on their equipment. The latest version of Cisco NetFlow is version 9. However, version 10 is standardized as IP Flow Information Export or IPFIX as defined in RFC 7011.

To better understand how NetFlow works, we first need to define a flow. A flow is essentially a communication between hosts on an IP network. The conversation or traffic transfer will comprise multiple packets. A switch or router running NetFlow or IPFIX, will keep a dynamic flow table referred to as the flow cache, where new flows are added to the table and old ones aged out. When a packet enters the switch or router, it is inspected to see if it's part of an existing flow by referring to the flow table. If it is not in the flow cache, the IP header is inspected, and a new entry added to the flow cache. The following IP packet attributes are inspected to define a flow and flow cache creation is illustrated in figure 11-1:

- IP source address
- IP destination address
- Source port
- Destination port
- Layer 3 protocol type
- Class of Service
- Router or switch interface

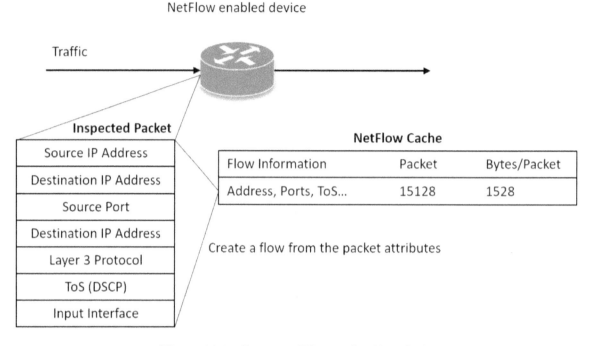

NetFlow enabled device

Traffic

Inspected Packet

| Source IP Address |
| Destination IP Address |
| Source Port |
| Destination IP Address |
| Layer 3 Protocol |
| ToS (DSCP) |
| Input Interface |

NetFlow Cache

Flow Information	Packet	Bytes/Packet
Address, Ports, ToS...	15128	1528

Create a flow from the packet attributes

Figure 11-1, Creating a Flow in the Flow Cache

Eventually, traffic transfer between hosts will cease. If traffic within a flow is not detected after a period, the flow is removed from the flow cache.

There are four basic elements to make up the NetFlow system. They are as follows:

- The NetFlow Monitor
- The NetFlow Exporter
- The NetFlow Collector
- The NetFlow Analyzer

Figure 11-2 illustrates a basic NetFlow system

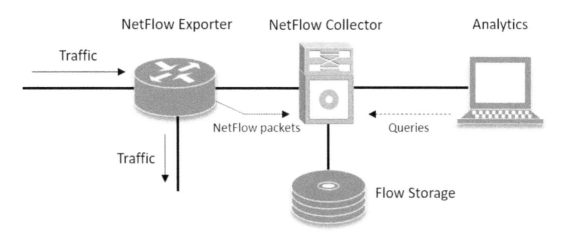

Figure 11-2, A Basic NetFlow System

The NetFlow Monitor is the configuration assigned to the ports on the switch or router, which probes the ports and creates the flow records. The exporter is also located on the switch or router, and is responsible for the communication with and data transfer to the collector. Flow records are transferred to the collector, which is essentially a historical database of flow records. There will then be some software application used that can process this data and produce the desired reports.

So NetFlow is a useful tool to characterize the traffic flow on IP networks and this in turn can help a network administrator make the necessary changes to deliver the desired QoS. Cisco NetFlow v9 was essentially standardized within RFC 7011 as IPFIX.

RFC 2544 Throughput Testing

RFC 2544, Benchmarking Methodology for Network Interconnect Devices, was standardized in 1999. This old methodology was designed to be used in lab environments for testing the performance of a network device. Tests would be set up as illustrated in figure 11-3 and figure 11-4.

Figure 11-3, RFC 2544 with Single Test Unit

Figure 11-4, RFC 2544 with Dual Test Unit

A single tester can be used to send and monitor RFC 2544 traffic and the Device Under Test (DUT) would somehow loop back the RFC 2544 traffic. An alternative is to use a dual tester, where one end sends RFC 2544 traffic and the other end monitors the RFC 2544 traffic after it has passed through the DUT.

The test measures the amount of data a device could pass (throughput), frame loss, frame errors and latency (frame delay). Frame sizes are set at the following rates for Ethernet: 64, 128, 256, 512, 768, 1024, 1280, 1518 bytes. You will notice there is no IMIX value that would represent a mix of frame sizes for real traffic. The final setup task is to set a test duration and to monitor the results. RFC 2544 does have some deficiencies as a standard when applied to real networks, the first being that test traffic is UDP based, whereas most data traffic is TCP based. There are testers which can set up TCP based test traffic, but their TCP implementations often do not behave like TCP would in real network environments. By far the biggest drawback of RFC 2544 is that it is not network CoS aware, nor does the test environment represent the contracted Service Level Agreement a customer may have. Y.1564 addresses these issues and is discussed next. However, RFC 2544 has one major benefit in that it is simple to use an operate. Test heads are often built into Carrier Ethernet equipment and it is therefore cheap to implement. Thus, you will often find that a Service Provider would prefer to run a simple RFC 2544 test at the contracted service rate to quickly check service performance, rather than implement more complex technologies such as Y.1564 or TWAMP.

One final consideration is that RFC 2544 is intrusive. RFC 2544 tests can be run at line rate and so excludes all other traffic. Likewise, the application of a loopback can cause data traffic to be cut off.

Y.1564 - Ethernet Service Activation Test Methodology

The first point of note is that Y.1564 measures service performance at Layer 2 only and is designed purely for Ethernet services. Y.1564 addresses some of the shortcomings of RFC 2544 by allowing each QoS class associated with a service to be tested independently as well as together. RFC 2544 is not service class aware.

Parameter	Real-Time (voice video)	High Priority	Best Efforts
CIR (Mbps)	10	40	5
EIR (Mbps)	0	60	95
Frame Delay (ms)	5	15	30
Frame Delay Variation (ms)	1	n/a	n/a
Frame Loss Ratio (%)	0.001	0.05	0.1
VLAN	100	200	300

Table 11-3, An Example SLA assigned to Three Service Classes

When a service provider offers a carrier Ethernet Service there may well be multiple service classes. Typically, one for voice or video, one for assured forwarding and one for best efforts. Each service class will have a contracted Service Level Agreement (SLA). Typical parameters of an SLA will be maximum Frame Loss Ratio, Maximum Frame Delay, maximum Frame Delay Variation, Committed Information Rate and Excess Information Rate, an example of which is shown in table 11-3. Frame Delay Variation is akin to jitter in timing networks. Simply put, it is the difference in delay between current frame and the previous frame (essentially: variation in delay). With

Y.1654, the business SLA parameters can be mapped in the Ethernet device in very much the format the customer has in their contacted SLA. Y.1564 is then able to use a built-in line rate test-head to test the service against those parameters and publish a performance report. Since Y.1564 is often run as a service commissioning tool, this report is often referred to as 'birth certificate'. The tests can be run as one-way tests or as two-way (round trip) tests. Time synchronization will be needed between end nodes for one-way tests.

Y.1564 has two test phases. These are the Service Configuration Test and the Service Performance Test.

The Service Configuration Test Phase

The methodology behind the Service Configuration Test phase is that each class is tested in turn. The network administrator will set up the number of test iterations they want to execute and the duration of each iteration, and the system will then step the test traffic rate up to the peak rate (often the line rate) based on the number of iterations. For example, if the service has a CIR of 400Mbps and EIR 400Mbps (peak rate will be 800Mbps in this case) and the operator wants 10 test steps, then each step will be 100Mbps. The first test is at 100Mbps and the final will be at 1000Mbps. This concept is illustrated in figure 11-5, which shows a test period of 20 seconds per step.

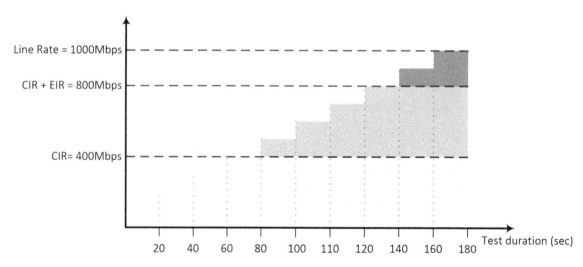

Figure 11-5, A Service Configuration Test Example

When the Service Configuration Test runs, it is only looking to register if frames transmitted up the CIR are received within the maximum loss ratio specified in the SLA. These frames are marked green. With MEF compliant Ethernet services, frames transmitted at a rate over the CIR but less than the peak rate, are colored yellow. There is no guarantee that these frames will be transmitted to their destination and so the Service Configuration Test will not fail if yellow frames are lost. The Service Configuration Test can transmit frames above the peak rate to ensure that they are discarded by the network and that no frames marked red are received. Once a Service Configuration Test has completed for one class, the next is tested in turn until every class has been tested.

The Service Performance Test Phase

Once the Configuration Test phase has completed, the Service Performance Test phase commences. Essentially, each CoS is tested simultaneously to ensure that the network delivers the contracted service level. Bear in mind that only frames colored green need be delivered. The test duration is configurable, but should be run long enough to ensure that service delivery is reliable.

Y.1564 Challenges

The concept of Y.1564 is sound, but the challenges occur from an operational perspective and adoption is low amongst Service Providers. The fundamental issue is that Y.1564 is complex to set up and operate. Some implementations do have graphical aids and wizards that help, but we do have to remember to look at this from the perspective of the operative in a Network Operations Center (NOC). Y.1564 requires that the SLA parameters are added to network elements to test against. SLAs can be complex, comprising Frame Delay, Frame Delay Variation and Frame Loss parameters. The technology used to measure Frame Delay, Frame Delay variation and Frame Loss can also be complex to setup. Y.1731, discussed later, is often used for this, along with a line rate test head for The Service Configuration testing and Service Performance testing. Often, a simple RFC 2544 based test at the contracted service rate is good enough and far simpler to manage.

Y.1731: OAM Functions and Mechanisms for Ethernet Based Networks

So far in this chapter, we have built up a picture of what QoS measurement technologies are available at the port level and what are intrusive in nature for creating a service birth certificate. We now need to consider what is available for in-service 24/7 SLA measurements for both Layer 2 Ethernet and Layer 3 IP services. If we focus on Layer 2 Ethernet services first, then the ITU specification, Y.1731, is the technology most widely deployed in modern carrier Ethernet networks.

Y.1731 provides several Operations Administration and Maintenance (OAM) functions. Some of these functions simply monitor an Ethernet Virtual Connection (EVC) to see whether or not it is working. We, however, will take a closer look at the functions designed to provide SLA measurements. Specifically, Y.1731 can measure round trip delay, one-way delay, dual and single ended frame loss and frame delay variation. We will now take a closer look at how Y.1731 provides these measurements.

Y.1731 Terminology

Y.1731 defines an operational model for Ethernet service OAM. An Ethernet service will comprise a customer domain, a provider domain and an operator domain. The customer will install their own equipment, as will the provider and the operator. The Y.1731 operation model describes how each of the Ethernet service domains interact with each other to provide end to end OAM as shown in figure 11-6.

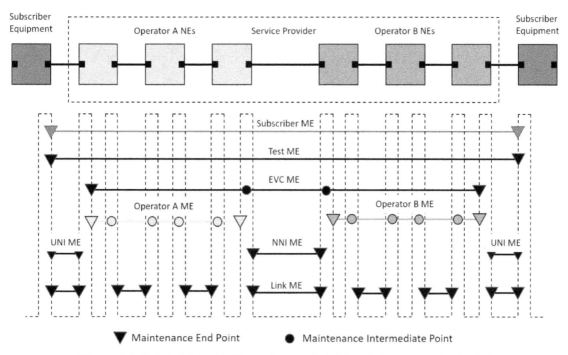

Figure 11-6, The Y.1731 Operational Model for Ethernet Service OAM

First, we need to define a Maintenance Entity (ME). An ME is an entity that requires management and it is bounded by Maintenance Endpoints (MEPs). The devices within the ME make up the Maintenance Entity Group (MEG) and the MEG is generally the service to be monitored. MEGs are monitored at different levels based on whether the MEG forms the subscriber MEG, the service provider MEG or the operator MEG.

A more formal definition follows. A MEG includes different MEs that satisfy the following conditions:

- MEs in a MEG exist in the same administrative boundary
- MEs in a MEG have the same MEG Level
- MEs in a MEG belong to the same point-to-point Ethernet connection or multipoint Ethernet connection

For a point-to-point Ethernet connection, a MEG contains a single ME. For a multipoint Ethernet connectivity containing 'n' endpoints, a MEG contains $n*(n-1)/2$ MEs.

For performance monitoring, we only need to consider a definition of a MEG End Point (MEP). A MEG End Point marks the end point of an Ethernet MEG which can initiate and terminate OAM frames for fault management and performance monitoring.

MEGs operate a given level. There are 8 levels in total and operators tend to use the lower levels from zero upward. The provider will take mid to highest levels, for example 3 to 5 and the customer will take the highest levels say 6 to 7. This is a convention and not fixed by a standard, but the operator must setup Y.1731 at a level lower than the provider and the client must operate at a higher level than the provider, if they plan to interoperate using their Y.1731 instances. It is worth noting that The Metro Ethernet Forum (MEF) has published Service OAM Fault Management Implementation Agreement in MEF 30. This sets out a scheme for MEG level assignment as described in the table 11-4.

MEG	Default MEG Level
Subscriber MEG	6
Test MEG	5
EVC MEG	4
Service Provider MEG	3
Operator MEG	2
UNI MEG	1
ENNI MEG	1

Table 11-4, Default MEG Levels as Defined in MEF 30

Now that we have a basic understanding of Y.1731 terminology we can look further at how the protocol provides performance reporting metrics.

EVC Availability

Y.1731 provides a simple means to verify whether an EVC is in or out of service. Let's take a simple point-to-point EVC. The service instance is defined by the MEG. The MEG will have two end points associated with the User to Network Interfaces (UNIs) at each end of the service. Y.1731 will simply insert a Continuity Check Message (CCM) into the EVC. The CCM is a single Ethernet frame, periodically transmitted form one UNI to the other. The frequency of CCM transmission may be as high as 3.3ms or as high as low as 10 minutes. The receiving UNI knows the CCM frequency and if 3 consecutive CMMs are lost, then the EVC is deemed to be out of service. CCM messages are unidirectional and so transmit and return paths are monitored independently. CMM messages are also multicast and so multipoint Ethernet service can be monitored in the same way.

A point-to-point or E-LINE service may comprise more than one EVC per UNI. To ensure that the CCM frame is injected into the correct EVC, it uses a concept called a primary VLAN, where frames crossing the UNI into the Service Provider domain will be mapped to the EVC by a VLAN member list. One of these VLANs (called the primary VLAN ID) is assigned to the CCM frame. This ensures that the CMM, too, is mapped to the EVC. For frame loss, however, you will want to count all other customer frames that enter that EVC. Therefore, a VLAN member list is associated with the Primary VLAN. The concept is illustrated in figure 11-7. CMM messages within Y.1731 are called ETH-CCM.

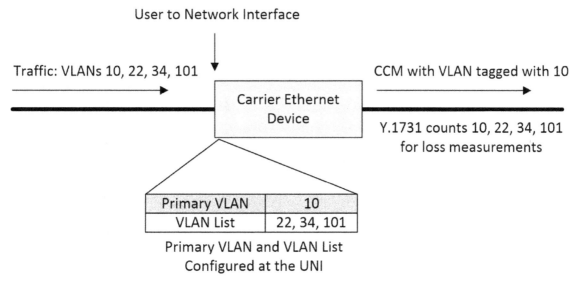

Figure 11-7, Primary VLAN Associated with ETH-CCM Frames

Y.1731 Delay Measurements

We have a basic understanding of Y.1731 MEGs and MEG End Points at the UNI. If we can inject CMM frames between the UNIs, then why not add timestamp information to the frame to provide a simple mechanism to measure round trip delay and one-way delay. The timestamp information in Y.1731 is equivalent to the time representation format in format in IEEE 1588-2002. Thus, we can measure delay to microsecond granularity.

Figure 11-8 illustrates the principle of one-way Y.1731 delay measurements.

A delay measurement is initiated from the source UNI. In Y.1731 terms, this is referred to as an ETH-DMM frame. A frame sent in response is called an ETH-DMR frame. TxTimeStampf is the timestamp at the transmission time of the ETH-DMM frame. RxTimef is the time that the receiving UNI receives the frame. One-way delay is calculated using the following formula:

One Way Frame Delay = RxTimef – TxTimeStampf

It must be noted that both the sending and receiving UNIs must be time synchronized for one-way delay measurements. If this is not possible, then only round-trip or two-way delay measurements can be monitored.

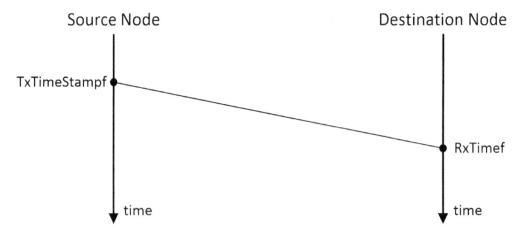

Figure 11-8, One-way Y.1731 Delay Measurements

Figure 11-9 illustrates the concept of two-way or round-trip delay measurements.

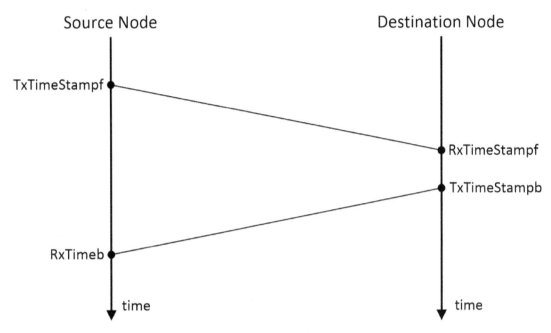

Figure 11-9, Two-way Delay Measurements

For two-way delay measurements, two additional timestamps are added to the ETH-DMR frame. These are the time that the ETH-DMM frame was received by the receiving UNI and the time the ETH-DMR frame was transmitted. This mean that the sender can deduct the processing time at the receiver from the total round-trip delay. Round delay measurements do not need time synchronization. Round-trip delay measurements are calculated as follows:

Two-Way Frame Delay = (RxTimeb – TxTimeStampf) – (TxTimeStampb – RxTimeStampf)

Y.1731 Frame Delay Variation

Frame Delay Variation is akin to jitter within a timing network. However, with Frame Delay Variation, we are looking to calculate the difference between the delay of the current compared to the previous frame. The service frames must belong to the same CoS instance on a point-to-point EVC. The same ETH-DMM and ETH-DMR frames are used for Frame Delay Variation and Frame Delay calculations. Since we are only dealing with relative difference between consecutive frames, then time synchronization between end points is not needed for either one-way or two-way Frame Delay Variation measurements.

Y.1731 Frame Loss Measurements

ETH-LM procedure is an ITU-T Y.1731 procedure that can be used to periodically measure Frame Loss Ratio of an EVC. Measurements are made between two MEPs belonging to the same ME.

These measurements are based on actual service frames exchanged between the two external interfaces. Frames must be 'in-profile' - in-profile meaning frames which are transmitted within the Committed Information Rate or are marked green. There is no necessity to deliver frames transmitted over the Committed Information Rate or those marked yellow, so these are not counted for frame loss measurements. That said, some Ethernet equipment does allow out-of-profile frames to be counted.

The procedure for loss measurements involves a Controller MEP sending an ETH-LMM (Loss Measurement Message) once per time interval (e.g. 1 second, 10 seconds, 1 minute) to a Responder MEP. The Responder MEP replies with an ETH-LMR (Loss Measurement Reply). The messages are used to collect the counts of the number of service frames transmitted and received by the two MEPs in a point-to-point MEG. LMM PDUs are sent to the unicast address of the Responder MEP at the MEG Level of the ME.

The calculation is done entirely by the Controller MEP and is referred to as a 'single-ended procedure'.

For each ME for which a loss measurement procedure is configured, an MEP maintains two local counters for each peer MEP in its MEG and for each CoS ID.

- TxFCl: Counter for in-profile data frames transmitted towards the peer MEP
- RxFCl: Counter for in-profile data frames received from the peer MEP

These messages must traverse the same path as the service frames belonging to the monitored EVC. The CoS ID of the ETH-LMM is set to match the monitored CoS ID.

When several CoS IDs are to be measured, a separate procedure is run for each CoS ID.

112

The Controller MEP sends the following counter in the ETH-LMM PDU:

- TxFCf – Copied from the local TxFCl

The Responder MEP generates an ETH-LMR PDU in response, containing:

- TxFCf: Value of TxFCf copied from the ETH-LMM frame
- RxFCf: Value of local counter RxFCl at the time of ETH-LMM frame reception
- TxFCb: Value of local counter TxFCl at the time of ETH-LMR frame transmission

Upon reception of the ETH-LMR, the Controller MEP performs the FLR calculation for both ends for the time interval t_c-t_p (Where t_c is the current time and t_p is the last sample time). The formulae for these calculations follow:

$$\text{Frame Loss}_{\text{far-end}} = |\text{TxFCb}[t_c] - \text{TxFCb}[t_p]| - |\text{RxFCb}[t_c] - \text{RxFCb}[t_p]|$$

$$\text{Frame Loss}_{\text{near-end}} = |\text{TxFCf}[t_c] - \text{TxFCf}[t_p]| - |\text{RxFCl}[t_c] - \text{RxFCl}[t_p]|$$

The advantage of using ETH-LMM and ETH-LMR frames is that they are used to measure the loss of real traffic. However, they only work for point-to-point EVCs. Another potential issue is that a service may not be passing any traffic and if this is the case, although no losses will be flagged, there is no way to ascertain whether the service is actually experiencing frame loss.

Y.1731 Synthetic Loss Measurements

Y.1731 ETH-LMM and ETH-LMR calculations only work for point-to-point traffic. Y.1731 does, however, provide a mechanism for measuring frame loss in multipoint topologies and where no traffic is being transmitted. This mechanism is referred to as Synthetic Loss Measurements (SLM).

As implied by the name, synthetic frames are injected into the EVC and are transmitted to peer MEPs. It is these frames, rather than real traffic, that are counted to measure data loss and as such, any measured loss is deemed to be a statistical measure of what real frame traffic will be.

Y.1731 ETH-SLM frames collect counters to maintain a count of transmitted and received synthetic frames between a set of peer MEPs. Y.1731 ETH-SLM is used to perform on-demand tests by sending a finite number of frames with ETH-SLM information to one or multiple peer MEPs and similarly, receiving frames with ETH-SLM information from the peer MEPs. Each MEP then performs frame loss measurements which contribute to unavailable time.

The procedure involves a Controller MEP sending an ETH-SLM once per time interval to a Responder MEP, to which the Responder MEP replies with an ETH-SLR frame. The messages are used to collect the counts of the number of ETH-SLM and ETH-SLR frames transmitted, and the number of ETH-SLM and ETH-SLR frames received by the two MEPs. ETH-SLM PDUs are sent to the unicast address of the Responder MEP at the MEG Level of the ME.

For each ME for which an SLM procedure is configured, an MEP maintains two local counters for each peer MEP in its MEG and for each CoS ID.

- TxFCl: Counter for in-profile SLMs transmitted towards the peer MEP
- RxFCl: Counter for in-profile SLRs received from the peer MEP

These messages must traverse the same path as the service frames belonging to the monitored EVC. The CoS ID of the ETH-SLM is therefore set to match the monitored CoS ID.

When several CoS IDs are to be measured, a separate procedure is run for each CoS ID.

The SLM message includes the following counter:

- TxFCf – Copied from the local TxFCl

The Responder MEP generates an ETH-SLR in return, containing:

- TxFCf: Value of TxFCf copied from the ETH-SLM frame
- RxFCf: Value of local counter RxFCl at the time of ETH-SLM frame reception
- TxFCb: Value of local counter TxFCl at the time of ETH-SLR frame transmission

Upon reception of the ETH-SLR, the controller MEP performs the frame loss calculation for both ends for the time interval t_c-t_p (Where t_c is the current time and t_p is the last sample time).

$$\text{Frame Loss}_{\text{far-end}} = |\text{TxFCf}[t_c] - \text{TxFCf}[t_p]| - |\text{TxFCb}[t_c] - \text{TxFCb}[t_p]|$$

$$\text{Frame Loss}_{\text{near-end}} = |\text{TxFCb}[t_c] - \text{TxFCb}[t_p]| - |\text{RxFCl}[t_c] - \text{RxFCl}[t_p]|$$

The IETF Two-Way Active Measurement Protocol (TWAMP)

Y.1731 can be used to measure network performance for Layer 2 service only. The protocol PDUs do not have any IP header that will allow them to be routed. In simplistic terms, TWAMP can measure the same network performance metrics as Y1731, but for Layer 3 IP services. TWAMP is defined in RFC 5357 and updated in RFC 8545.

TWAMP is a standard protocol framework that separates sessions based on the client and server architecture. The TWAMP client is a network host that initiates the TCP connection and acts as a control-client and a session-sender. The TWAMP server is a host that acknowledges the TCP connection and performs the roles of a server and a session-reflector. TWAMP-Control messages are exchanged between the control-client and the server and TWAMP-Test messages are exchanged between the session-sender and the session-reflector. This arrangement is shown diagrammatically in figure 11-10.

TWAMP consists of two interrelated protocols: TWAMP-Control and TWAMP-Test. TWAMP-Control is used to initiate, start, and stop test sessions, whereas TWAMP-Test is used to exchange test packets between two TWAMP entities.

TWAMP can measure round trip and one-way delay, one-way and two-way packet delay variation, packet loss ratio and continuity check. The format of the timestamp for delay measurements is the same as in RFC1305 (Network Time Protocol v3) and is as follows: the first 32 bits represent the unsigned integer number of seconds elapsed since 0h on 1 January 1900; the next 32 bits represent the fractional part of a second that has elapsed since then. Consequently, this will provide microsecond granularity for delay measurements. Like Y.1731, time synchronization is only needed for one-way delay.

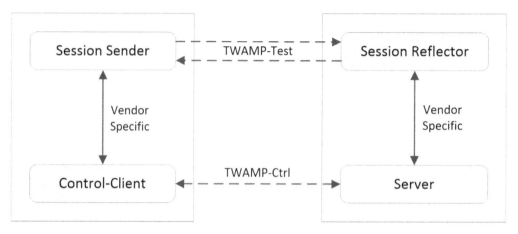

Figure 11-10, TWAMP Test Flow

In a TWAMP test flow the TWAMP-Control performs the following:

- Sets up the TCP Connection
- Performs an optional integrity check
- Issues TWAMP-Control commands
- Starts and stop TWAMP sessions

The TWAMP-Test performs the following:

- Sender: sending and receiving probe packet
- Reflector: reflecting probe packets

Summary

Within this book we have looked at the evolution of QoS from the early days of Time Division Multiplexing to the DiffServ model generally applied to today's packet switching networks. We have seen how TDM networks evolved into circuit switching networks to provide growth and convergence but, unfortunately for them, proved expensive in comparison with Ethernet networks. We have also explored how, at the same time, IP had become the dominant Layer 3 routed protocol, meaning that business drivers lead to packet switching technologies becoming prevalent and replacing Circuit Switched networks in the converged voice and data space - this drive being further reinforced by the growth of the Internet.

We have also looked at how IntServ was one of the first initiatives to address the problem of QoS over packet networks, but suffered from scalability issues associated with RSVP when deployed in large Service Provider networks. It also was reliant on making IP packet-based networks behave like circuit switching networks by signaling paths in advance – a problematic approach, since networks often re-converge and data paths change dynamically. IntServ was then abandoned in favor of the DiffServ model as it eliminated all signaling and the problematic RSVP. However, IntServ triggered much work on traffic classification, congestion avoidance, and queuing and scheduling. IntServ is important because of the legacy it created and much of the resultant technology is still used today in DiffServ applications.

Now, as convergence becomes a reality and enterprises are driving the demand for lower cost, higher bandwidth networks, Ethernet is fast becoming a ubiquitous medium. Work within the Metro Ethernet Forum is aimed at turning this enterprise class technology into a carrier medium. The MEF has developed QoS specifications that are built into many MEF compliant Ethernet products.

The idea that Circuit Switched behavior can be engineered into Packet Switched networks is a compelling one, since this behavior makes the job of applying QoS much easier. We see carriers, especially, deploying traffic engineering in the form of IP MPLS and MPLS-TP to do this very job. There is a new technology now that could displace MPLS with the complex signaling needed to engineer traffic and this technology is Segment Routing.

Networks are evolving and we took a brief look at SD-WAN and some of the QoS challenges that this technology faces.

Therefore, as it stands, today all the elements are in place to provide low cost, high bandwidth, converged networks that support the latest and most robust QoS mechanisms.

Glossary

ABR	Available Bit Rate
AF	Assured Forwarding
API	Application Programming Interface
AS	Autonomous System
ATM	Asynchronous Transfer Mode
ATSC	Advanced Television Systems Committee
BFD	Bidirectional Forwarding Detection
BGP	Border Gateway Protocol
CBR	Constant Bit Rate
CBS	Committed Burst Size
CB-WFQ	Class Based – Weighted Fair Queuing
CCM	Continuity Check Message
CD	Compact Disc
CF	Coupling-Flag

CIDR	Classless Interdomain Routing
CIR	Committed Information Rate
CoS	Class of Service
CPE	Customer Premises Equipment
CRC	Cyclic Redundancy Check
CS	Class Selector
CSPF	Constrained Shortest Path First
DS	Differentiated Services
DSCP	Differentiated Services Code Point
DSL	Digital Subscriber Line
DUT	Device Under Test
DVB	Digital Video Broadcasting
DVD	Digital Versatile Disc
EBS	Excess Burst Size
ECMP	Equal Cost Multipath
EF	Expedited Forwarding
EGP	Exterior Gateway Protocols
EIR	Excess Information Rate
EVC	Ethernet Virtual Connection
EXP	Experimental Field
FCS	Frame Check Sequence
FEC	Forwarding Equivalence Class
FEC	Forward Error Correction
FIFO	First in First out

FTP	File Transfer Protocol
GAL	Generic Alert Label
GRE	Generic Routing Encapsulation
HDLC	High Level Datalink Communications
HTTP	Hypertext Transfer Protocol
IEEE	Institute of Electrical and Electronics Engineers
IETF	Internet Engineering Task Force
IGP	Interior Gateway Protocol
IMIX	Internet Mix
IP	Internet Protocol
IPFIX	IP Flow Information Export
IS-IS	Intermediate System to Intermediate System
IT	Information Technology
ITU	International Telecommunication Union
JSON	JavaScript Object Notation
IPX	Internetworking Packet Exchange
LAN	Local Area Network
LDP	Label Distribution Protocol
LER	Label Edge Router
LIB	Label Information Base
LLC	Logical Link Control
LLQ	Low Latency Queuing
LSP	Label Switched Path
LSR	Label Switches Router

LTE	Long-Term Evolution
MAC	Media Access Control
ME	Maintenance Entity
MEG	Maintenance Entity Group
MEF	Metro Ethernet Forum
MEP	MEG End Point or Maintenance End Point
MIB	Management Information Base
MPLS	Multi-Protocol Label Switching
MPLS TE	Multi-Protocol Label Switching Traffic Engineering
MPLS-TP	Multi-Protocol Label Switching – Traffic Profile
MTU	Maximum Transmission Unit
NFV	Network Functions Virtualization
NIC	Network Interface Controller
NOC	Network Operations Center
OAM	Operation Administration and Maintenance
OSI	Open Standards Interconnection
OSPF	Open Shortest Path First
OUI	Organizationally Unique Identifier
PCE	Path Computation Element (or Element)
PCR	Peak Cell Rate
PDH	Plesiochronous Digital Hierarchy
PGPS	Packet-by-Packet Generalized Processor Sharing
PHB	Per-Hop Behaviors
PHP	Penultimate Hot Popping

PIR	Peak Information Rate
PPP	Point-to-Point Protocol
PQ-CBWFQ	Priority Queuing with Class Based Weighted Fair Queuing
PVC	Permanent Virtual Circuit
QoS	Quality of Service
QR	Quick Response
RAID	Redundant Array of Independent Disks
RED	Random Early Detection
RFC	Request for Comment
RIP	Routing Information Protocol
RMON	Remote Network Monitoring
RSVP	The Resource Reservation Protocol
RSVP-TE	Resource Reservation Protocol - Traffic Engineering
SCR	Sustainable Cell Rate
SD-WAN	Software Defined Networking in the Wide Area Network
SDH	Synchronous Digital Hierarchy
SDN	Software Defined Networking
SLA	Service Level Agreement
SMTP	Simple Mail Transfer Protocol
SNMP	Simple Network Management Protocol
SONET	Synchronous Optical Networking
TCP	Transport Control Protocol
ToS	Type of Service
TWAMP	Two-Way Active Measurement Protocol

UBR	Unspecified Bit Rate
UDP	User Datagram Protocol
UNI	User to Network Interface
VBR	Variable Bit Rate
VLAN	Virtual Local Area Network
VLSM	Variable Length Subnet Mask
VPLS	Virtual Private LAN Service
VPN	Virtual Private Network
VXLAN	Virtual Extensible LAN
WAN	Wide Area Network
WFQ	Weighted Fair Queuing
WRED	Weighted Random Early Detection
WRR	Weighted Round Robin
XML	Extensible Markup Language

About the Author

Gary Hallberg has over 33 years of experience in the telecommunications and data communications industries. He started his career working with Circuit Switched voice and data technologies in PDH and SDH environments and then moved on to work with early Packet Switched networks using Frame Relay and ATM. His career shifted focus to IP routing when the Internet started to grow, designing large scale service provider networks using leading edge equipment from vendors such as Juniper and Cisco. Gary attained Cisco Certified Professional status during this time. Presently, he is working for a global equipment vendor with a focus on Ethernet networks and is at the forefront of network evolution, providing infrastructures for SD-WAN, Network Functions Virtualization, SDN and 5G backhaul. Gary has a Bachelor of Engineering degree in electronic engineering and a Master of Philosophy degree in robotics and manufacturing.

www.ingramcontent.com/pod-product-compliance
Lightning Source LLC
LaVergne TN
LVHW081346050326
832903LV00024B/1341